APPETIZERS
AND
MAIN MEALS
FOR THE MODERN
FAMILY

APPETIZERS AND MAIN MEALS FOR THE MODERN FAMILY

CHEF FRANK OROFINO

authorHOUSE®

AuthorHouse™
1663 Liberty Drive
Bloomington, IN 47403
www.authorhouse.com
Phone: 1 (800) 839-8640

Published by AuthorHouse   04/17/2015

ISBN: 978-1-5049-0670-8 (sc)
ISBN: 978-1-5049-0669-2 (e)

Library of Congress Control Number: 2015905637

Print information available on the last page.

TO MY DAUGHTER

MY DAUGHTER WOULD KILL ME IF I DID NOT MENTION HER IN THIS COOK BOOK SO HERE WE GO DAWN.

TO MY PRINCESS, THIS COOK BOOK IS DEDICATED TO YOU, AFTER ALL SOMEONE HAS TO TEACH YOU HOW TO COOK. YOU ARE MY PRINCESS AND HAVE BEEN SINCE YOU WERE BORN.

YOUR BOUT WITH CANCER AT AN EARLY AGE MADE YOU STRONG, WHAT WITH EVERYTHING YOU WENT THROUGH THEN. YOUR STRENGTH PULLED YOU THROUGH ALL THE CHALLENGES A YOUNG PERSON IS CONFRONTED WITH.

MY LOVE TO YOU ALWAYS PRINCESS

YOUR POPPY

DEDICATED TO MY LOVE

TO GRANDMA

I remember when I was very young watching my grandma cooking and remembering the delightful smells that she produced out of her kitchen. The smells just made my mouth want to taste everything she was making, and I never knew why that was. Being young all I thought about was eating my grandma's food. The love she put into all her dishes were a touch of beauty. You have to remember that old world grandmas no matter what country they came from never wasted a thing. It was food of the night and then leftovers during the week. But for some strange reason grandma always made us feel like it was a new day and a new dinner. As I grew older I wanted to cook next to my grandma so she had my grandfather make me a stool that I could be higher on the stove and help my grandma. My mother today will tell you that the only one that can make her marinara sauce is me. My love for cooking is a delight for me and the people that enjoy my food. I have so many good friends that wait for me to cook. To my grandma who is long gone from this earth but as my mom would say she is always in our hearts.

THANK YOU GRANDMA FOR YOUR LOVE OF COOKING AND FOR YOUR LOVE FOR YOUR FAMILY

REMEMBERING THE GOOD TIMES AND THE GOOD YEARS

I remember years ago at an early age the lessons both my grandparents taught me, my grandma for teaching me the cooking skills of her generation and the lessons learned by my grandfather of using a hammer, screwdriver and other tools. The man could fix anything; he even fixed shoes in early days for my mother and the rest of their children. That was the way of the old school and the lessons that they brought to all of us. Don't be foolish, save your money for a rainy day.

I remember the aroma of the kitchen when grandma cooked, there is no way you can physically describe what aroma passed through the entre house during the holidays. I remember my mother and grandmother starting to cook early in the morning for the family that will be arriving that day. Dinner at 1:00 and then leftovers at 5:00. And in the mist of all this cooking was a 6 year old boy looking and helping in any way I could to learn the history of Italian cooking. My grandmother was so patient with me taking the time to teach me the skills and the knowledge of her cooking. To this day I cook the same recipes and through the years have developed my own skills in cooking all different types of food.

The tastes and smells of gravy, meatballs, sausage pork and pepperoni cooking in a big pot were incredible. I couldn't wait until she gave me the chore of stirring the gravy, and when she wasn't looking grabbing a piece of Italian bread and dipping it into the pot of gravy. Yes of course she was watching but never said a word.

The fresh fish, the home made pasta, all on a board that my grandfather made her years ago. The board is still used by my mother, I know the board is older that dirt. But the love that that old wooden board brought to the family years ago and still today I believe that it makes the perfect pasta. She had everything so arranged for dinner that food came to the table hot and smelling like a fine restaurant. When you feed a family during the holidays of 30-40 family members there was no disputing that grandma had everything well in hand.

It was like watching a movie made in Italy and observing a family getting together during the holidays and everyone talking at the same time and trying to keep up with 5 different conversations at one time. I have no idea how the women did this but it was incredible to watch and listen. And here is my grandmother sitting next to her husband taking this all in and saying to herself this is what family is all about. Even if she had no idea about the conversations, all she had to do was to look around the table at family members that at times did not get along through the year, become a total family built on the respect of both mother and father and grandparents.

To her that meant everything. Through the years until her death in the 60's that how I remembered our family. With both grandparents gone the family seems to split and there was no more visiting the grandparents on a Sunday for that special dinner.

What happens to the family, why did grandparents keep the family together, was it the history of them, their age or maybe just that we had the respect for them not to disappoint them because of the love they had always given us.

Yes times have changed, but give me that simple life of years ago versus today. Both parents working because of cost, the fine cars, the big expensive homes and the keeping up with the Jones's next store. Why wasn't that an issue when we were growing up? The computers, the hand held games, big screen TV's, and the biggest of all these is that little thing growing out of the ear the famous phone in the ear.

Have you ever been in a crowd and a cell phone rings and everyone is reaching for their phone and finding out it wasn't theirs. Why do we need to be in contact with everyone each minute of the day, we eat breakfast, lunch and dinner with a cell phone either stuck in our ear of one right next to us? What are we waiting for the natural disaster of the world, what would we do, call everyone and let them know I wouldn't be coming over for dinner tonight. Now don't get me wrong I have also a cell phone and I do believe in one for emergencies. I have used it for that, but to have one stuck in my ear, there are times when I walk down the street I see men and women talking to them and screaming and yelling at themselves only to find a phone stuck in their ear.

I thank God that growing up with my grandparents we had none of that. We talked one on one with each other, and yes we had a phone but, ok times have changed, but is it for the good. Do we still communicate one on one eye to eye or just by phone and oh yes via e-mail. The system that allows you to talk to someone without them knowing that you are making faces at them or really do not like them but because you work with them, they have more money than you, they take vacations to expensive place. You get my drift.

Can you ever imagine for Christmas giving your grandparents of years ago a computer or phone. Just imagine.

Now kids with cell phones, not going there. Now to get back to the reason behind my thoughts of childhood and growing up with grandparents.

As you can tell I am not a famous book author, just a plain and simple Italian man who has grown up with the precious memories of living with grandparents.

You talk about food, I remember one day my grandfather going to the fish monger (the local fish market) and buying snails (escargot to the fancy people). The key he said is to keep them in cold water the night before they are cooked with a weighted lid to keep them inside. Well he did not have a heavy enough lid and in the middle of the night I heard something rattling and you guessed it, the snails raised the lid and began crawling out of the pot and onto the walls and into the sink. My grandfather was always the first one up each morning, except that morning when I arose first to see the snails all over. He came in and said don't tell your grandmother what happened. He laughed, picked up all the snails and put them back in the pot and this time put a heavy pot on top of the lid.

That night sitting down and eating snails in gravy, I thought back to that morning and looking at my grandfather laughed and he winked at me. One of many precious moments that have become the greatest memories of my life.

My grandfather coming over from Naples, Italy, area where he was a Carabinieri, or a policeman, in his younger days. He decided to make a life in America which he was so proud to call his future home. My mother who now is the rock of the family has so many memories of the family in her younger days of relatives all living under one roof. Keep in mind we never owned a house for all my life and here we lived in an apartment where to this day 89 years later she is still in the same apartment third floor up. The memories that apartment has from over 75 years is incredible. The house it self is over 120 years old and still sturdy as a rock. I remember my grandfather making wine, lemon limoncello and grampa in the basement with the wood ceiling cracking under the load of the press for the wine. When relatives came over from Italy and a relative was living in a house or apartment it was expected that the family coming over would live with them until they found a job and a place of their own. At one point in time my mother told me that there were five families living in this apartment complex some on the top floor by me and the others on the first and second floor.

It wasn't hard to open your house and your heart to family at those times, everyone pooled their money together to make sure that everyone had clothes and food was always on the table. We were never a rich family in money but a rich family in spirit, love and the togetherness in family. And what times they were. The men going out to work with lunch pails consisting of fruit, cheeses, tomatoes and home made bread. Yes always home made bread. My mother told a story one day about when my grandfather went to work and the other workers was comparing their lunches they always asked my grandfather, Frank what do you have for lunch. He always shared his lunch with his fellow workers that are the type of man he was.

He was the most gentleness of men, a loving husband, and father and of course a loving and helpful grandparent. What is so strange about what I am writing is that I at times can never remember what I had the day before, what I did the day before, but can remember every little detail about growing up with my grandparents.

I remember one time years ago my grandfather bought piece of land in New Brunswick, New Jersey, he wanted a place to take his wife and children. He starts to build his dream shack, he would find nails and straighten them out, boards that he could use for the house, and he finally built this dream house for his family. The way the story goes from my mother is that one weekend he took every one of his children and wife to New Brunswick to show case his pride and joy, well my grandmother asked my grandfather where the bathroom is and he replied the old house out back. My grandmother responded back to him that she will not come to this house until my grandfather built a bathroom inside this house. Which he did because his wife wanted one. He never argued with that he just said in Italian yes dear, sounds familiar doesn't it. The farm as he called it wasn't very big, about 2 acres, but being the man he was, farmed that land with love and desire and what that land produced for the family was incredible. He plowed, weeded and cut all by hand, to him that was thanking the earth for the giving of life.

The house now had a bathroom and kitchen and two bedrooms and a small living room, but the nights sitting under the grape vines that he brought back from Italy, the actual true green grape was incredible. He dug a well and had a hand pump attached and an old case iron tub to catch the water, running the fruit and vegetables under the water and then eating them was pure heaven. At night sitting under the grape vines you would pick some grapes are you were sitting there and enjoy the sweetness of the grapes.

Next door we had a farmer, Farmer Brown I think there is one in every town, anyway each morning on the weekend he would send me over to him to purchase fresh milk and fresh butter for that weekend. Boy the government health department would go crazy over that, but ha it didn't hurt our health any. My grandfather would say the fresher the food the better for you. I remember him starting a purple fig tree that he brought over as a seedling and from that one tree that he planted in the yard at home he grew 10 or 12 tress for his farm. Remembering when they were young trees, at fall we would go up to the farm and purchase fresh cow manure, screens, tar paper and buckets. He would line the tress with the tar paper, them put the screen around that and then create a pocket in between the tree and the tar paper and guest who had to fill the tree up with the cow manure, you got it me.

As grandpa would say you treat all life as God would treat life and it will serve you always and he was right, each spring we would go up to the farm and unwrap all the tress and the leaves and buds would be growing as if to say thank you grandpa for treating so good during the winter. Each year the trees would give him more and more fruit and each year he would thank all the tress by preparing them for those cold winter months.

The weekends at the farm was where dreams came true for the grandparents and the entire family. The women cooking and the men helping grandpa out with odd jobs that he couldn't do on his own. The family was rewarded with great company, great food and most of all the love and support of the entire family. The kids playing on an old tire that hung from this big old tree, the swing that he made from old wood and rope was just what the doctor ordered for a fun family time on the weekend.

My older cousins use to kid me, because I grew up and lived with our grandparents and they use to say grandma and grandpa's spoiled grandson. I remember when I use to go up to the farm with just my grandfather he uses to pick me up after school on Friday and we headed via buses and trains to the farm. I couldn't wait to get there. I had my own bed to sleep in so naturally when the weekends came for the entire family I had cousins that were older than me that wanted to sleep in the bed, well that was not going to happen, so my one cousin, Connie had to sleep in the crib. To this day at 59 years old still do not live it down.

I remember my grandfather building two out houses one for storage and one as an outside kitchen in which he found an old wood burning stove. The food that came out of this stove was so incredible that my grandmother always cook on this stove. Especially the fresh killed chickens tasted so good.

That reminds me of another story, when I was about 9 or 10 years old, and we were at the farm, my grandfather was going to teach me how to kill a live chicken, so being the trustworthily lad that I was with him I decided ok teach me. So here I am he gets a string and ties one end to my arm and the other end to the legs of the chicken. Now he explains on the proper procedure for killing a live chicken, failing to mention what the chicken will do once I cut off its head, so here I go and the next thing I know here I am with a chicken still moving and the chicken attached to my arm. What a mess as you can imagine.. But it was good to see him laugh at me and telling me what to do. But when grandma came out after hearing all the noise it wasn't laughter anymore from grandpa.

If I could have had one more day with my grandparents over more money or fame, I would take that in a minute. How many children now days can remember stories like that? Today it has become a race for time about sports, computers, and computer games and now the biggest fad is an Ipod. What is the big deal with an Ipod, something sticking out your ear and listening to music rather than listening to the natural world's beauty around you? And some of the music now, yes I am an old 40's, 50's and 60's fan but that music said something good, not most of the music now a days. I feeling am if I cannot understand what they is either talking about or singing about it's not worth listening too. Yes that's me being and old man if you want to classify me as that. I love to dance I remember at an early age my mother teaching me the 2 step, fox trot, and jigger bug.

Look at the dances today, kids dance 20 feet apart and shack like they have something inside their pants. The strange thing about that is when I am out dancing on the dance floor and the what I call the younger generation see that, they come up to me and ask teach me that looks so romantic, especially the young women, so we maybe getting to them with the soft music of our time and maybe not they just look upon us as old people that do not understand the younger generation.

The younger generation, not going there, they are our future and hopefully will make the world a better place to live.

I remember going to weddings and gatherings and I would be the only young boy dancing on the dance floor. Do you remember the CYO dances what fun, remember 2 hands apart or at your high school dances the teachers watching over us, something like the movie Grease? And the hot rods of our day, muscle cars and cruise nights on a Friday and Saturday night. The A&W stands, White castle hamburgers, where we all went to show off our cars. Girls in shirts with bobby socks, and the guys in white tee shirts with cigarette folded on the side of our sleeves. Stick back hair or crew cuts. Something to say about us also, but I think we have more memories of enjoying our friends honestly than now a days, but that is only my option.

I know that we always want to give our children better than what we had, but is it the right way, I remember my first job when I was 13, in fact a side story, when I was about 9 years old we have what we called then and A&P market similar to what the big food chains are now. I had a little red wagon and use to stay outside and ask the people can I take your groceries home for you and they would give me a tip for doing that. Well mothers day was coming up, so with the money I saved for carrying groceries home, that mothers day I walked up to the flower store and purchased a corsage for my mother. I guess it wasn't the best of flowers being the money I had, but my mother cried and said that was the prettiest flowers she has ever received. There was just something that day that made me realize that family is everything and the mothers loved are true and honest. Of course my grandmother in her immortal way winked at my mother and said to me when Frank were is mine, I thought about it a minute and said grandma I love you with all my heart but this is mom's day, and with that she gave me the biggest hung and kiss.

As time went on in my youth with my grandparents, I always thought I would have them around forever, but on day on a Saturday, my life changed. I was 13 years old and woke up that Saturday morning to noises and cries for help on the phone, I got up and went into my grandparents bedroom to find my grandfather gasping for air, I remember getting into bed with him and saying pop everything will be fine at that moment, my grandfather passed away in my arms. At 13 you have not experienced death and all I knew is that my

Grandfather fell asleep in my arms so he was going to be alright. Not true, my mother took me away from my grandfather and I fought with all the strength I had not to leave him. All I could remember was calling out poppy, poppy, but no answer.

My mother sat me down and explained that grandpa passed away, and not realizing it I said to her well when he is coming back, of course deep down inside I knew what had happened but would not realize it. I question to her was why did God take my grandpa away from me, what did I do to have that done, in her beautiful way now don't forget this was her father, but in a soft voice and not showing any emotion said to me, he will always be with you son its just that God has a special assignment for grandpa, and I said what was that, and she replied to watch over the entire family for the rest of our lives. It seemed right at the time but as the years went on I knew better that mom was just trying to comfort me.

I will not go into the funeral part, if you are an Italian you will know what I mean of years ago funeral. My grandmother of course did not take it very well in fact about 3-4 years later; she missed her husband so bad that she developed a chest infection and was in the hospital dying. At that point the entire family was at the hospital, babies and all and one at a time my grandmother called each one of us in, children, son, daughters, son-in laws and daughter-in laws and said her good byes.

I was the last to good in with my mother; she turned to me and explained that she all of us so very much, but it was time to go see her husband that she missed so very much. Being older now I understood what she needed to do, I hugged her so tight and kissed her so much and I said to her, grandma I will miss you so much, my life will never be the same but go and give grandpa a big hung and kiss for me when you see him.

She looked at both me and mom who by now was taking it very bad and said I and pop will always be with you. Love each other as we have done and what we will still be doing. And with that, she closed her eyes took her one last breath and with a smile on her face fell asleep for ever. I know at that point than grandpa came and got her and would have a happy after life together. I kissed her for one more time and said my good byes.

Her funeral was worse than grandpa's enough said about that.

Enough of the sad times lets get on with the happy times and memories. I remember the time at Christmas that my parents bought me a set on Lionel trains under the tree, well through the years I added on to the set and before you know it I was unable to put the set under the tress. Now keep in mind that my bed room which my mothers brother of 6 years older stayed there also. Well one day before the holidays my grandfather made two wooden horses and a piece of plywood and we started to assembly the train set in the bed room. It took up most of the space, but to see the joy on his face in helping me with setting this up and watching the fruits of out labor we would watch the trains run for hours upon hours. The smoke from the engine, the missile launcher, the crossing gates, all the lights, even my mother made the town with the people and the cars and all.

A Happy Time

The memories we have of those days with our grandparents, it's not like today. No matter what ethic background you come from, the grandparents were the life blood of the family. The excitement of knowing that we are going over to grandma's house to visit them and to have dinner there was a treat. Grandma would sneak each one of us aside and give us so money and told us not to tell our parents. It wasn't much but at that time that cared, it was a present from grandma. Grandma would show her love to each and everyone one of us. She had no favorites we all were the twinkle in her eye. When grandma seen us coming up the stairs, her eyes lit up and her arms were out stretched to hug and kiss each one of us with the same love she had for her entire family.

You see grandparents do that because that's all they know, to give love and affection to each member of their family. Grandpa, well that's a different story, underneath that husky body with white hair and shiny white teeth, was a gentle soft spoken Italian from outside of Naples Italy. Yes speaking about his pearly white teeth, grandpa used to smoke the old black Italian cigars that you could smell for miles, in fact when grandma wanted grandpa, she used to say to me Frankie go and find grandpa, all I had to do was go in the direction of that smelly cigar and there he was. Speaking about his teeth, grandpa use to brush his teeth with Ajax cleaner, to keep his teeth white because of the tar from the cigars, he brushed them so much that he wore off the porcelain off his teeth, but they were sure white.

In the morning grandma used to get up and make coffee for everyone and my father could never figure out why the coffee at night was much milder and tasted better than the morning coffee. Being a wise Italian after the breakfast coffee was done, grandpa would take the coffee grinds put them on a brown paper bag, spread them out and let them dry out in the sun and that night he would use some of them to blend in with the new coffee beans. Grandpa always had tricks up his sleeves that came from making the food and money last longer. See they never squandered money like we all do now. If we do not finish everything we just throw it away.

Good example, kids with soda or in other states pop, when they are finished drinking the soda and ever notice that there is always either a half or less in the can, they never finish it.

Try this today, at dinner time you ate what was put on the table that grandma made for us. There was no such thing is saying to grandma or especially grandpa, I don't like this or I am full and leaving food on your dish, to them that was being wasteful, then you got the sermon from grandpa on how hard they work to put the good food on the table and they were right, so you thought about it and finished everything that was on your plate especially knowing that grandma made desert, so see if you didn't finish your meal, you had no desert and no snack at night because you didn't eat your super.

I remember as I grew and started to become a young man my grandmother and mother use to sit me down and explain the finer things of life. I could remember at an early age my father taking me to restaurants and teaching me how to address myself at a restaurant. What to do and how to order, of course no liquor, how to sit and the use of the utensils at the table. I always remember that and to this day I still remember what Dad taught me. Getting back to the lessons of grandma and Mom, how to act, how to treat a woman and of course what not to do. I have taken the lessons learned and apply them to this day. I passed these lessons on to my children to this day.

Don't get me wrong, I have nothing against the kids of today, but you have to admit the styles that they are wearing are a little bit funky. Yes in the 60's we also, but to pay $100.00 for a pair to torn and cut jeans sound a bit crazy. Why can't they buy a pair of $20.00 jeans and cut and tear them and save money. And the ear rings, body rings and as I call them the external and internal rings. I could never imagine eating with a big fat ring stuck to my tongue. I think today it's more of a statement that they are part of what is called the new generation or the click. It's amazing to see young people dressed up or to them dressed up and going into a fine restaurant with torn jeans and bagging pants. Oh baggy pants, what's with that? You see these young men walking down the street and always pulling up their pants because they are ready to fall down, or the crotch of the pants hanging down to the floor. What's up with those $200.00 sneakers, 100.00 jeans, $50.00 tops, you would think that they would be at the height of the fashion world. Yes I guess I am getting old, but that is not the way to present you. To me the way you present yourself is the way people will look at you. Yes the young ones of today don't care what people say, but I hope to see in my life time these young people being senators, congressman and women and walking into the Capital building and speaking about the things that made America what it is today and what we need to change.

Now we get to the one topic that drives me up a wall. Tattoos, what's up with that? Don't they like their bodies? Now I am not talking about the little tattoos that look very nice in certain areas of a woman's or mans body, it's the tattoos that run the entire length of a human body, all colors and all designs, some good and some that I just do not know why. I figure it this way, what do you do when you get tired of the tattoos, do you just peal them off, I think not, and what happens down the road if they want to remove them, can you imagine getting them off your entire body. I know I went off the beaten track, but its something that came into my mind. So where was I? The finer things in life.

I remember when I was 13 and I started working across the sheet in a used car lot, I wanted to learn the mechanics of a car, engine and all that went with it. I used to come home with grease up to my eye balls and my grandmother use to tell my mother, but why does he have to get so dirty. My mother explained to her that this is what he wants to do. I just it broke my grandmothers heart to see me dirty. She used to scrub my clothes until all traces of grease and dirt was gone. That's my grandmother. I also remember that my Uncle Nick's brother use to deliver coal in those times to homes and I helped him deliver coal also. Imagine coming home to your grandmother with coal all over you. I think that is what broke the camels back. On Saturdays my job was to clean the three flights of steps before I went to bowl on a Saturday. I didn't mind that at all. It was my job given to me by my grandmother.

It's funny how you never questioned the jobs that your grandparents gave you, you just said yes and did the job as best you could. They instilled a sense of pride in doing things and wanting do please them in ever way you could. There was never a question or refusal in anything they wanted. It was always yes grandma or grandpa. After all it's better to say yes than have to deal with a no from grandpa. You can imagine what would happen.

After my grandfather sold the farm in New Brunswick, he found a little piece of land across the railroad tracks in Jersey City. He built a little shack and you could never imagine how much vegetables he grew from the little piece of land. Grandpa always had to be close to the land, I think that's why I enjoy it so much. When it was time to pick to fruits of his labor, we all went down to that little piece of land crossed the railroad tracks and started to bring all the vegetables in baskets to the car. Of course grandpa couldn't have picked a piece of land close to the tracks, no it had to be the best spot where the sun would reach all his crops. So lugging baskets of vegetables across those tracks was a job in it self besides watching out for the occasional trains that were passing by.

My grandmother and my mom and sometimes I would help them jar the tomatoes and vegetables that he grew. That was my introduction to canning. I had already at the age of 6 started helping my grandmother cooking. My grandfather had to make me a stool so I could be able to reach up to the stove and see and help her. My love for cooking came straight from my grandmother. She taught me the true meaning of Italian cooking and the love that goes into it.

I consider myself to be a go cook, and from her teachings I have improved and cook just about anything. Everyone that I know enjoys my cooking and says you need to open your own restaurant. I would love to do that, if I did I know what I would name the place, **Annette's** after my grandmother. I cook old world Italian dishes, the same as my grandmother had done for many years. In fact my mother to this day says I cook better that her and my food is the same as grandmas. That make me feel so good and every time I cook a recipe of my grandmother I think of her.

Its funny how the brain works, sometimes it hard for me to remember what I a week or even a day ago, but I can remembered years back of my grandparents and the things they taught me. I guess it's the love and the caring that will always stick in my mind with them. To this day when ever I go back to visit my mother I always have to go to the cemetery and visit their grave site and talk to them, tell them how much I love them and truly miss them. And yes to have one more day with them would mean the world to me.

They are always with me and in my heart, and in everything I do. When things go bad I pray to them to help me and when things go right I tell them thank you for being by my side.

The apartment I lived in to this day my Mother still lives there, it's about 75 years that she has lived there and each time I go back the memories of that apartment is just filled in the air in every room. To this day when I go home and drive down the little side street of Lembeck Avenue I can still see my grandmother looking out of the kitchen window. She passed away many years ago, but to this day I still can see here face each and every time I drive down that street and to this day I will always wave at her from the car. I always expect that when I open the door in the front of the building and start walking up the two flights of stairs she will greet me at the door. The memories are so strong in that house that you feel that grandma, grandpa and now my Dad who recently passed away are all there.

There are so many memories; it's not hard to remember. I don't remember the relatives of years ago because I wasn't born then but the ones I remember hold a special place in my heart. Down stairs on the second floor is where my Aunt Jean uses to live. This Aunt was on my grandmother's side, my nick name for her was barrel belly, and I guess you can put two and two together on that one. She was so funny, every night she came up to our apartment, she was so quite coming in that she scared everyone when she turned the corner of the kitchen to come into the TV room. Everyone use to jump and scream. She was the life of a party and made everyone laugh. She use to say bad words in Italian and made my grandmother laugh. Everyone was so use to her expressions that rather than holding your breath and saying that wasn't nice, just laugh, you couldn't help it.

Getting back to the family, there were so many relatives, nieces and nephews, sister-in-laws, brother-in-laws, cousins, grand kids, and people from Italy that can over from the other side, it would be to hard to mention. As you can tell at holiday time everyone gathered at grandmas. And grandma would love this. She would always say my family is here.

Relatives from both sides of the family would gather around at any time to feast on grandma's food, and she never disappointed anyone on her food. Except for one time that I can remember. Her son Frank, as you will see there are many men named Frank in our family, so some of us had nick names, I will keep mine in my head for now. Anyway, her son was going out with a fabulous girl named Jackie. One night Massaro that was his last name and also his nick name because of all the Frank's in the family, brought Jackie to the house for dinner, now Jackie wasn't Italian so in her mind she would think this was going to be a normal dinner. NOT.

So grandma proceeded to serve dinner, there was some normal Italian food but that main meal consisted of sheep heads and sheep brains. Well I wish I have a camera then when Grandma put this big plate of heads and brains on the dinner table. The expression on Jackie's face was, well I wish I had a camera. So here we all were eating the meat around the jaw of the head and eating the brains that grandma fried in olive oil, what's the problem to this day they are both a delicacy and you can still find then in the old market places. Even high class restaurants still serve the brains, they are called a different name but they are still brains. It was a fun night. The entire time my grandfather was watching Jackie eat and after the night ended, my grandfather turned to my grandmother and said, what was wrong with Jackie, meaning why she didn't eat everything. My grandmother turned to my grandfather and explained to him that she doesn't eat lamb. I knew from the expression on his face that that was the truth, but my grandfather just smiled and went on his business. After that not sheep heads or brains was served to us while Jackie was there for dinner.

Well as the years went on the memories went on also. I remember going to the shore with mom, dad grandma and grandpa when I was young. I remember mom and grandma under an umbrella all day and my grandfather playing with his grand kids that were there. Grandpa was always good with us kids and he always showed his love for each and every one of us no matter who it was. He had no special one, well yes he did me. Well you have to remember I lived with them since I was born and left to join the service when I was out of high school.

Unfortunately with the death of my grandparents, the family slowly drifted away from the house. Yes I know the kids got older they have kids and the rest is history. I just hope that they hold the memories as close to them as I hold them in my heart and mind. My daughter Dawn was very close to grandma even at that early age. In fact when Grandma passed away, to this day she has a star that she reflects on and says hi to Grandma. Now with the death of her other grandma and then my Dad who was very close to Dawn now have a star. It's imagining she can pick out each star for each one. I hope she has a star picked out for me when I go which I hope isn't soon. My two kids mean the world to me. At an early age they both experienced the pains of a divorce. My daughter went through a bout of cancer at 12. She was so brave, she fought for her life and I am so proud of her. In fact her mother told her, Dawn thank God you are like your father to fight like this, I think through our divorce that was the only nice thing she has said. But who knows she was probably angry, I know she was.

My son Mark is great, he has become a very handsome man and has a great built, just like his dad. I love them both so much. Yes it was hard on Mark also, for a time we were not close, and that's to be expected he was very young. Now we are starting to enjoy each other and I love him to death.

With the passing of their grandfather who was very close to him, they became the pillows of strength of their grandmother. And my son-in-law also John who will do and has done anything for them.

I am so proud of them and I love them with all my heart. Don't ask me how I got on this; it's just whatever comes into my mind at the time of the family.

The family, like every family there are good times and bad times, but the bad times go away and the good times stay with us forever.

I remember I was always into mechanics; I followed the space program when I was young, played marbles, collected baseball cards. I know you don't remember but I built a two wheel skate box. Let me explain that. You get a 2" x 2" piece of wood cut it to about 4-6 feet long. Now you get a skate, you know the ones you use to clamp on your shoes take it apart and remove the rubber insert so the wheels will tilt from side to side so you can steer the wood. Now you get a wooden crate, the one that soda came in. Now you mount the skates to the wood, mount the wooden box to the other side of the wood right up front. Attach two pieces of smaller wood on angles so you can hold on and steer. Now you get bottle tops yes bottle tops and on top of the box design any design you want.

Now you take your finish skate board, yes we had skate boards before anyone else did, find a big hill and do it to it. The fun was seeing who can go the fastest and still stay on the board. No, no helmets, knee protection or gloves, why. Thinking about it now with the injuries we all had it might have been a good idea.

We had all sorts of games when we were young, marbles, draw a circle in the dirt each of us would put marbles in the circle and we all had our favorite what we called our shooter marble that we used. The trick was to shot your marble from outside the circle and what every marbles went beyond the circle you kept. Each time you hit a marble outside the circle you went again until you couldn't get a marble outside the circle. Then it was the other guys turn.

Baseball cards, we use to trade them, flip them up against the wall and who ever was the closest to the wall won those cards. Then we use to flip, you had to match the other guys card, if his card was face up or face down you had to match that or you lost.

Stick ball, getting a broom stick and buying a Spalding high bounce ball. This was played on a side street with sew plates. What I mean by that is the sew plate in the center of the street was home base.

Then you mark first, second and third bases. You had a pitcher, catcher and out fielders in the center of the street not on the side walks. You had to hit the ball on the first bounce, three strikes and you are out. It was cool because with the high bounce ball you could put spins on the ball that reacted different each time. It was not a matter on throwing the ball straight. That was too easy.

Then we had box ball, yes I said box ball. This was done on the same side street but in a square. The only rules were you had to hit the ball with your palm and had to keep it within the box square of the street.

Yes we had football and baseball and basketball, we didn't live in the Stone Age. But the baseball games were fun. And at times we did break some windows in homes.

FUN TIMES WITH FUN MEMORIES

Please understand I am not an author for books that people enjoy and I might skip around the family memories, but as they come into my mind I write about them.

The years with grandma and grandpa extremely loved, I remember growing up and speaking Italian, now you have to understand I was in the process of going to the first grade in my time there was no kindergarten. My mother at one point told my grandmother to stop talking to me in Italian and speak in English. Can you imagine going to a Catholic school and speaking Italian? I thought that was my language.

School that's another story, I was a patrol boy that is someone who worked with a policemen to direct the kids to cross the streets when they were allowed. It was ok, it good me out of class early. Yes I was an alter boy also and had to perform my duties at an early mass because that was the mass my grandmother went to. I remember her looking at me and feeling so proud so I could not disappoint her so I kept doing the early mass.

Grandma was very religious, in fact every Friday there was no meat on the table it was all fish and we were not allowed to eat anything before Sunday mass because of the rules of the church. The school and church was St. Paul's and the church was very beautiful until the pastor of the church decided to remodel the church. We had Stations of the Cross that I remember an old man for hours at a time standing and painting with great detail all the Stations of the Cross. The church was as I would say an old gothic design with statues and the alter was so beautiful especially at the holiday season. But now here comes a pastor that is going to change everything and white washed the Stations of the Cross, moved the alter into the center of the church with a simple alter and removed the pews and put just simple chairs. When my grandmother seen this for the first time, I cannot explain to you her emotions. Needless to say for a long time she never went back to church in fact she explained her emotions in Italian to the pastor. Thank god he didn't understand Italian.

The teen years, what an experience. When I was 13 years old I started working in a used car lot across the street. The name of the place was Lembeck Auto. The owners name was Joe Roselle but we called him Lucky, not because of his lucky streak, but just because. I started out as all young kids do on their first job was cleaning, polishing and vacuuming the cars, putting out trash and cleaning the garage after all the mechanics repaired the cars. A highly technical position I held with pride. It was fun and I made money, after awhile Lucky started me out on the basics of auto repair, checking oil levels, and finely working my way up to starting up the cars. Then he progressed me to changing the oil, and oil filters, brake repair and some body work. I remember coming home very dirty and my Grandma use to tell my mom, but was does he have to work there is gets so dirty. My mom replayed to her that's what he wants to do. Not line my grandma's son Massaro, remember his name was also Frank, all he wanted to do was play baseball. If you ask his sisters to this day they will reply they al spoiled him. He never got dirty and never wore jeans. I remember that on a Saturday morning I had to sweep and clean the two flights of stairs before I could go and bowl in the league. As I was cleaning the steps, Massaro would leave to play ball. Talk about getting off track with this.

Anyway when I turned 15 years old Lucky gave me a new job, it was taking the cars and moving them in spots that me wanted, Talk about luck, my first encounter in driving skills. I did fine and loved to drive the cars. At that time the old cars are now considered classic cars. Can you imagine if we knew at that time that these cars would be worth something one day? He used to let me take a car and go to the store, pick up parts and go to the motor vehicle for plates and registration along. Keep in mind that I was only 15 years old and to drive legally in New Jersey at the time you had to be 17 years old. What a treat. Of course my parents never knew this. The best car I love to drive especially in the summer was a 1957 Thunderbird convertible, light blue outside and white interior. I was king, radio blasting and just cruising. Never entered my mine, if I got stopped by the police what could happen, but Lucky knew all the cops in Jersey City and he did allot of favors for them so, well you take it from there. On the east coast we have Sabrette hot dog stands on the corners. These hot dogs are the best; they are the east coast favorites. Well one day Lucky turn to me and said we have to make a trip down the road, get the truck and we started to drive. We arrived at an auction and I asked him are you buying cars, he replied just wait. All of a sudden he started bidding on a hot dog cart, I was a little confused and I asked him after he purchased the cart and loaded it on the truck why did he buy it. His reply was we are going to set it up on the street by the car lot and I can sell hot dogs and make extra money. I thought extra money in my pocket sounds pretty good to me. Well you could say he financed my business to open the stand. Now he I was cooking hot dogs, warming up onion sauce, sauerkraut and stocking with soda and oh yes YOO HO.

YOO HO you don't know what YO HO is, well let me tell you, it's a chocolate drink that is still made and it is the best drink to drink with Sabrette hot dogs, to this day when I go and visit my Mom I go down to the next City, Bayonne and on 25th street there is a vendor who has been there for years that still sells them. So I go in order 4 hot dogs mustard and onions and two YO HO's and proceed to eat the dogs and the drinks. When dad was alive, I use to go to Bayonne and I had better bring him back at least two hot dogs mustard and sauerkraut or I was in the dog house. Of course with his sugar problem he couldn't eat them but my mother never said a word, she seen how much pleasure it gave dad to eat them. And yes the next morning his sugar would be high, but she never said a word.

Getting back to the hot dog stand, here I am hot dogs are ready, soda cold, onions and kraut ready, now all I needed was customers, I am going to make a fortune, NOT. Everyone who came to see Lucky was, Frank get these guys some hot dogs and soda, its on me, so I figured the first day lucky is helping me with getting customers for after so I didn't mind, well WRONG AGAIN.

Everyday I was handing out free dogs to his friends and not making a dime. The best part now here comes my father, great a sale, NOT, Frank get your Dad some dogs and soda, so I knew that that point this was not going to be a profitable business for me, oh well at least I was giving hot dogs away. But lucky always made up for it in my pay so I enjoyed that time.

When I first started to work at Lucky's he had a German Shepard named GEE GEE. This dog was big and blonde color. Everyone was afraid of her, but GEE GEE and I hit it off from the first day. We were inseparable. She and I grew up together. I trained her to sit out on the lot without a leash, sit, and bark when I wanted and to keep quite when I wanted. No one could ever give her a bath, except me. I use to say gee gee time for a bath, get over here sit and be good. And that's what she did. When I use to move the cars for Lucky she had to go in every car I moved, she was worried that I was going some place without her. At night I would go over to the lot and take her out for a walk, play with her for awhile and then go home. If I didn't go over at night you could here her bark, that meant I know you are at home take me out and play, which I did.

During the afternoon, my mother would open the window and call gee gee and tell her to get frank for his lunch. She would come over to me no matter what I was doing, grab my arm and pull me outside. I know she knew she was going to get some of my lunch. When I finally received my actual driver's license, I was now able to take any car off the lot and drive. And yes the thunderbird was the choice of cars, top down in the summer and Crouse. Sometimes I would that her, but most of the time it was me and my friends. And believe me when I came back to the lot she let me know that I left her so walking and playing with her no matter what time I came home was a must. Went I went into the service my father took over the responsibility of taking care of her, and they both got along great.

I remember the nights as a young boy sitting on the front door stoop in the summer, grandma, grandpa, mom, dad, and any other family members or friend that came around. My grandfather would give me money and across the street was a soda shop, and buy Italian ices for everyone. To sit outside in the summer and listen to the old folks talk in Italian was one of the happiest times in my life.

During the hot times in the summer we had no A.C. units, it was a matter of having all the doors opens, the windows and small fans. We never had to worry in those days of any strangers trying to get into the house. It was a peaceful time in those days, but again times change. Now we have security systems, several locks on the doors and everyone is suspicious of everyone. Alarms in our cars, stun guns, and any other items that would protect us from every one. It's a strains world out there now. No I will not go into that subject because it is a lose, lose situation. That's the world we made.

Getting back to the happy days, I remember my grandfather giving me money and a white porcelain pot and going down to the local bar and having them fill the pot up with ice cold beer. On the way home I use to suck on the foam on the way back home. I could hardly reach up to the bar I was so small at that time, so the bartender would come around the end of the bar fill up the pot and I was on my way.

There was a bakery shop, that during Thanksgiving we would take our turkey down there and they would cook it for us in their wood fire oven for a small fee. You can never imagine the smells that came out of that shop during that time. Dad and I would go back down there pick up the turkey and the gravy for home. Of course while we were there we had to bring home bread and pastries for the rest of the day. The family would arrive and the meal began at 1:00pm and of course being Italian we ate all day on turkey, cold cuts and pastries. At the end of the meals the men would sit in the parlor and smoke cigars and drink grandpa's home made wine watch a game and of course take a nap.

Grandpa's wine, he would make the wine in our cellar, not knowing the true taste of wines, I thought it was the best wine in the world.

He would also make grappa which was the residue of the leaves, grapes and seeds. This was a very potent drink that you chugged down and not a sipping drink. It was about 100 proof and believe you me after two you felt like you got hit by a freight train. He also made lemonjello which consisted of good vodka, lemons and water and sugar.

Grandpa took the peals of the lemons only about 14 lemons put them in a big jar and then pour the vodka over the lemon rimes and close the lid and let this infuse for about 14 to 20 days. The vodka turned yellow from the rinses. After that he would boil water and sugar together until the sugar melted, let it cool off and then strain the lemon peals from the vodka and mix the vodka and the water sugar together. This would be served cold in a cold small shot glass. This was addicting, it tasted good and an enjoyable drink. All the kids were allowed to only have a sip of his mixture, but the men actually had more than one at times. He would serve this with espresso coffee.

You know in your life there are some relatives that you remember so well. One relative was my Aunt Bertha. She was the most funniest of all the relatives. She had every one when we all had dinner at Grandma's in stitches with laughing. She would tell jokes, and just have so much fun with the family. She had a word she use to use that for the sake of this book I am reframing from telling you but the word was the??? Word. She was the only one who could use this word and get away with it with the family because she used it in such a way that it was funny. She was the only one that uses this word that made my grandmother laugh. And being a devoted Catholic was very strange to us. But ha it made her happy and laughs so we all went along with it.

Aunt Bertha loved life and the family; she always showed us love and affection when ever she visited the family. She was so much apart of our family that at ever gathering she would be there, and we use to say aunt Bertha what is the word and she use to tell us. My mom use to go crazy when she said the word but we all knew aunt Bertha as a kind and gentle person that wanted us to make us laugh.

Years later I had heard that one day she was walking out of a bakery shop in New York and was hit by a bus. She suffered much illness and to this day she cannot walk or speak very well. Still my mother keeps in touch with her, she is now in an assisted living with her husband nick and is doing much better. She will always ask for me when Mom is talking to her and when I am visiting Mom we will talk to her. She is getting better but will never be the same. We just remember Aunt Bertha the way she was. God bless you Aunt Bertha.

My mother is the guarding of the family, she has so many memories that one day my cousin wants to write a book about the family and he had asked her to help him.

My cousin, the actor, yes actor, his name is Frank Vincent and he has made movies and is now starring in the Sopranos. He was in Raging bull, Casino, and many others. He has also written a book called The Gentlemen's Gentlemen. It's a book on men and also he goes into some on his family and his years growing up.

My older years well lets not go into that, that's for another story. All I can say is I worked very hard all my life and have many good people in my life both men and women. Maybe some day I will write about my experience in life and the people involved in my life.

This is dedicated to Grandma and Grandpa. As the stone reflects from the entire family

ALWAYS IN OUR HEARTS. REST IN PEACE MY LOVES

Frankie

TABLE OF CONTENTS

DRESSINGS

SAUCES

MAIN COURSES

SOUPS

GAZPACHO SOUP

2 LARGE TOMATOES

¼ RED ONION

1/2 RED PEPPER

2 GARLIC CLOVES

¼ CUP CUCUMBERS

2 SLICES OF CRUSTY BREAD **(DAY OLD)**

1 TEASPOONS SALT

¾ TEASPOONS WHITE PEPPER

1/3 CUP SHERRY VINEGAR

2 CUPS OLIVE OIL

1/2 TEASPOON SCIRRACHA

PUT ALL INGREDIENTS IN THE BLENDER AND PROCESS UNTIL CHUNCKY. SERVE COLD

SMOKED POTATO SOUP

1 LB POTATOES

BOIL POTATOES IN SALTED WATER UNTIL THE INSIDE OF THE POTATO IS A LITTLE SOFT. DONOT PEEL POTATOES. COOL POTATOS DOWN IN COLD WATER THEN DRY THEM AND CUT IN HALF AND PUT THEM ON THE SCREEN PAN FACE DOWN.

SMOKE THE POTATOS IN A COLD OVEN FOR ABOUT 1 HOUR. WITH ANY SMOKE CHIPS YOU DESIRE **OR USE 1 TABLESPOON LIQUID SMOKE TO SOUP**

PUT THE ITEMS BELOW IN A POT TO SIMMER UNTIL SOFTEN UP

1 ONION CHOPPED

1 LEEK CHOPPED

1 CELERY CHOPPED

ADD BUTTER AND COOK ABOVE ITEMS UNTIL SOFT

THEN ADD POTATOES

1 1/2 QUARTS OF WATER

2 TBL CHICKEN BASE

BRING EVERYTHING TO A BOIL AND COOK UNTIL POTATOS ARE SOFT. THEN ADD

3 TABLESPOONS MALT VINEGAR

2 TEASPOONS WHITE PEPPER

1 1/2 CUPS HEAVY CREAM

SIMMER FOR ABOUT 30 MINUTS THEN PUREE FINE. YOU CAN TOP THE SOUP WITH ANY OF THE DRESSINGS IN THIS BOOK THAT YOU DESIRE. ITS YOUR TASTE THAT MAKES THE SOUP.

CRAB SOUP

½ CUP CHOPPED ONION

½ CUP CHOPPED RED PEPPER

½ CUP CHOPPED CELERY

COOK ALL INGREDIENTS IN 5 OZ OF UNSALTED BUTTER FOR 15 MINUTES OR UNTIL SOFT.

MAKE A ROUX WITH 5 OZS OF BUTTER AND 5 OZS OF FLOUR MIX TOGETHER AND ADD TO POT CONSTANTLY STIRRING FOR 5 MINUTES ON MEDIUM HEAT. THEN ADD THE FOLLOWING INGREDIENTS:

½ CUP SHERRY WINE

½ CUP WORCESTERSHIRE SAUCE

2 TABLESPOONS CRAB BASE

3 CUPS MILK

2 CUPS HEAVY CREAM

STIR CONSTANTLY ON MEDIUM HEAT FOR ABOUT 20 MINUTES SO BOTTOM OF POT DOES NOT BURN.

REMOVE FROM HEAT AND LET COOL. PUT MIXTURE IN BLENDER AND BLEND UNTIL SMOOTH.

COLD POTATO SOUP

2 SHALLOTS CHOPPED FINE

1 POUND GOLDEN POTATOES

2 TABLESPOONS BUTTER

¼ TEASPOON OF KOSHER OR SEA SALT

3 SPRIGS TYME & 3 BUNCHES PARSLEY WRAPPED IN CHEESE CLOTH AND TIED

1 CUP HEAVY CREAM

¼ TEASPOON WHITE PEPPER

1 TEASPOON MINCED CHIVES

1 TABLESPOON SHERRY WINE

PEEL POTATOES, WASH THEM AND SLICE INTO ½ INCH PIECES. MELT BUTTER IN A SAUCE PAN AND ADD THE SHALLOTS. COOK OVER LOW HEAT UNTIL SHALLOTS ARE SOFT ABOUT 3 MINUTES. DO NOT ALLOW SHALLOTS AND BUTTER TO GET BROWN. ADD 1 ½ QUARTS OF WATER AND BRING TO BOIL. THEN ADD 1 TABLESPOON OF SALT, THE HERBS IN CHEESE CLOTH AND THE POTATOES TO THE BOILING WATER. COOK FOR ABOUT 25 MINUTES OR UNTIL POTATOES ARE SOFT. REMOVE THE CHEESE CLOTH OF HERBS. BLEND THE SOUP WELL. ADD THE HEAVY CREAM AND BLEND AGAIN. ADD THE SALT AND PEPPER.

ALLOW THE SOUP TO COOL AT ROOM TEMPERATURE AND THEN REFRIGERATE IT FOR AT LEAST 3 HOURS. PUT IN BOWL AND SPRINKLE WITH CHIVES AND DRIZZLE THE TOP OF THE SOUP WITH SHERRY WINE

CAULIFLOWER SOUP

1 TSP CHICKEN BASE

2 TBL LOBSTER BASE

2 CUPS CUT CAULIFLOWER

1 SLICE OF COOKED BACON

3 SPRINGS TYME

2 GARLIC GLOVES

1 SHALLOT

2 CUPS MILK

1 CUP HEAVY CREAM

½ TSP SALT

½ TSP WHITE PEPPER

1 LB LOBSTER MEAT **(CAN BE PURCHASED AT YOUR LOCAL GROCERY STORE)**

SIMMER ALL INGREDIENTS EXCEPT LOBSTER IN SAUCE PAN FOR 20-30 MINUTES UNTIL CAULIFLOWER IS TENDER. DISCARD THE TYME. PUREE IN BLENDER UNTIL SMOOTH WHEN SERVING TOP WITH LOBSTER MEAT GARNISH AND FRESH TYME.

YOU CAN SUBSTITUTE CRAB MEAT, SHRIMP, SCALLOPS OR EVEN FISH.

SERVE HOT

TOMATO BISQUE

½ CUP BACON

1 CUP ONION

1 CUP CELERY

1 CUP CARROTS

ALL ABOVE GETS ROUGH CHOP

SWEAT INGREDIENTS IN 5 OZ OF BUTTER UNTIL SOFT. THEN AFTER 5 MINUTES. ADD 5 OZ FLOUR TO FORM A ROUX. PUREE IN BLENDER 1 CANS #10 ITALIAN PLUM TOMATOES AND ADD TO POT ALONG WITH 2 CUPS OF WATER AND 1 TABLESPOON CHICKEN BASE.

SIMMER FOR 30 MINUTES STIRRING OCCASIONALLY. ADD THE FOLLOWING INGREDIENTS:

1 TEASPOON KOSHER SALT

1 TEASPOON BLACK PEPPER

1 CUP HEAVY CREAM

1 CUP CHOPPED BASIL

LET COOL THEN PUREE IN BLENDER UNTIL SMOOTH.

SQUASH SOUP

1 ONIONS CHOPPED

1 ½ APPLES PEELED, SEEDED AND QUARTERED

2 ROASTED SQUASH

CUT SQUASH IN HALF LENGTH WAYS AND REMOVE SEEDS. PLACE SQUASH FACE DOWN ON PARCHMENT PAPER AND RUB SKIN WITH OLIVE OIL. BAKE AT 350 FOR 1 HOUR OR UNTIL SQUASH IS SOFT. REMOVE MEAT FROM SKIN AND PUT ALL ABOVE INGREDIENTS IN A POT WITH 6 OZ OF BUTTER. COOK UNTIL ONIONS AND APPLES ARE SOFT. THEN ADD THE INGREDIENTS BELOW AND SIMMER FOR 1 HOUR MORE.

ADD 1/2 QUART WATER

3 TABLESPOONS CHICKEN BASE

BLEND IN BLENDER UNTIL SMOOTH

TOP WITH MICRO GREENS AND BASIL / BUTTERMILK DRESSING

(RECEIPE FOR DRESSING ON PAGE 32)

SALADS

CRAB SALAD

1 HEAD BOSTON SALAD

1 LB CRAB MEAT **(DOES NOT MATTER WHAT TYPE OF CRAB MEAT)**

1 CUCUMBER PEELED, SEEDED AND CUT IN SMALL PIECES

1 AVOCADO CUT IN HALF LENGTH WAYS REMOVE THE SEED REMOVE THE MEAT AND CUT IN SMALL PIECES

1/2 TEASPOON KOSHER OR SEA SALT

1/2 TEASPOON WHITE PEPPER

1 CUP SIRRACHA MAYO

1 TABLESPOON PARSLEY CHOPPED

SIRRACHA MAYO CONSISTS OF 1 CUP OF MAYO AND 2 TABLESPOONS OF SIRRACHA. SIRRACHA IS A CHINESE HOT SAUCE CAN BE PURCHASED AT ANY GROCERY STORE.

ARRANGE LETTUCE IN A BOWL LIKE A CUP, ADD THE CRAB MEAT, CUCUMBER AND AVACOTO SPRINKLE WITH THE SALT AND PEPPER AND ADD THE MAYO. ADD THE PARSLEY

YOU CAN ADD LOBSTER MEAT IN SUBSTITUTE OF CRAB, SHRIMP, OR COOKED SCALLOPS.

COLD SEAFOOD SALAD

1 LB SHRIMP PEELED AND DEVEINED **(TAKE TAILS OFF)**

1 LB DIVER OR BAY SCALLOPS

½ LB MUSSELS

½ LB CLAMS **(CHERRY STONE CLAMS OR MAHOGANY)**

½ LB CALAMARI BODIES

3 STALKS CELERY CUT IN SMALL PIECES

1 CUCUMBER PEELED SEEDED AND CUT IN SMALL PIECES

2 LEMONS

½ TEASPOON KOSHER OR SEA SALT

½ TEASPOON BLACK PEPPER

1 CUP EXTRA VIRGIN OLIVE OIL

CLEAN AND DEBEARD THE MUSSELS. STEAM THE MUSSELS UNTIL THEY ALL OPEN UP. IF SOME DO NOT OPEN DISCARD THEM, DO THE SAME WITH THE CLAMS. LET THE MUSSELS AND THE CLAMS COOL. STEAM THE SCALLOPS FOR ABOUT 10 MINUTES AND AGAIN LET COOL. STEAM THE CALAMARI FOR 10 MINUTES AND AGAIN LET COOL.

AFTER THE SEAFOOD HAS COOLED ARRANGE THE SEAFOOD IN A BOWL, ADD THE CELERY, THE CUCUMBERS ADD THE SALT AND PEPPER AND SQUEEZ THE LEMONS. ADD THE OLIVE OIL MIX AND COOL IN REFRIGERATOR.

FENNEL AND MUSHROOM SALAD

1 BULB OF FENNEL CUT VERY THIN

2 CUPS MUSHROOMS CUT THIN (**RAW MUSHROOMS**) ANY TYPE IS FINE **REMOVE STEMS ON ALL MUSHROOMS**

¼ CUP SHALLOTS CUT VERY THIN AND SOAK IN WHITE VINEGAR FOR ABOUT 20 MINUTES THEN DRAIN AND ADD TO SALAD.

½ CUP SHAVED PIECES OF PARMISAM CHEESE **(TOP THE SALAD)**

½ TABLESPOONKOSHER OR SEA SALT

½ TABLESPOON WHITE PEPPER

3 TABLESPOONS LEMON PEEL **(YELLOW SKIN ONLY NO WHITE PITT)**

3 TABLESPOONS OF LEMON JUICE

½ CUP EXTRA VIRGIN OLIVE OIL

COMBINE ALL INGREDIENTS IN A BOWL, LESS THE CHEESE, SPRINKLE WITH SALT AND PEPPER ADD EXTRA VIRGIN OLIVE OIL. TOP WITH THE PARMISAM CHEESE.

WARM BACON & SHALLOT SPINACH SALAD

6 SLICES BACON

1 CUP BALSAMIC VINEGAR

1/8 TEASPOON WHITE PEPPER

1 SHALLOT CUT FINE

1 BAG BABY SPINACH

PREHEAT A SKILLET. CUT THE BACON INTO BIT SIZE SMALL PIECES AND PLACE IN THE SKILLET. COOK THE BACON UNTIL CRISPY THEN ADD THE BALSAMIC VINEGAR TO THE SKILLET ALONG WITH THE SHALLOT. REDUCE THE HEAT AND LET COOK FOR ANOTHER 5 MINUTES.

TAKE THE SPINACH AND PLACE IN A BOWL AND TAKE THE HOT BACON DRESSING AND POUR OVER THE SPINACH AND FOLD THE BACON DRESSING INTO THE SPINACH.

YOU CAN USE THIS AS JUST A SALAD OR PRESENT IT WITH ANY MEAT OR SEAFOOD DISH.

APPETIZERS

FRIED CALAMARI WITH A SPICY CHIPOTIE CHILI GLAZE AND PICKLED GINGER

1 POUNDS SQUID, RINSE IN COLD WATER THEN CUT INTO ¼ INCH RINGS

1 ½ CUPS ALL PURPOSE FLOUR

1 CUP PICKLE GINGER DICE IN SMALL PIECES **(GROCERY STORES WILL HAVE THIS IN A JAR)**

½ TEASPOON KOSHER OR SEA SALT

½ TEASPOON BLACK PEPPER

¼ CUP CHOPPED CHIVES

HEAT OIL TO 350 DEGREES. SEASON THE CALAMARI RINGS WITH SALT AND PEPPER. ROLL THE SQUID IN THE FLOUR TO COAT EVENLY. SHAKE OFF EXCESS FLOUR.

DEEP FRY AT UNTIL GOLDEN BROWN, ABOUT 2 MINUTES.

DRAIN THE SQUID ON PAPER TOWELS AND COMBINE IN A BOWL WITH ONE CUP OF CHILI GLAZE, DICED PICKLED GINGER AND CHIVES.

FRIED CALAMARI WITH MARINA SAUCE

1 POUNDS SQUID, RINSE IN COLD WATER THEN CUT INTO ¼ INCH RINGS

1 ½ CUPS ALL PURPOSE FLOUR

1 CUP MARINA SAUCE

½ TEASPOON KOSHER OR SEA SALT

½ TEASPOON BLACK PEPPER

HEAT OIL TO 350 DEGREES. SEASON THE CALAMARI RINGS WITH SALT AND PEPPER. ROLL THE SQUID IN THE FLOUR TO COAT EVENLY. SHAKE OFF EXCESS FLOUR.

DEEP FRY AT UNTIL GOLDEN BROWN, ABOUT 2 MINUTES

DRAIN THE SQUID ON PAPER TOWELS ARRANGE ON A DISH WITH A SIDE BOWL OF MARINA SAUCE FOR DIPPING.

MARINA SAUCE IS IN THE COOK BOOK OR USE YOUR FAVORITE SAUCE.

FRIED EGGPLANT

1 ITALIAN EGGPLANT

3 CUPS ANY BREADCRUMBS

3 CUPS VEGATABLE OIL

3 OUNCES OLIVE OIL

3 TABLESPOONS CAPERS

1 TABLESPOON KOSHER OR SEA SALT

¼ TEASPOON BLACK PEPPER

¼ CUP CHOPPED BASIL

¼ CUP SHAVED PARMESAN CHEESE

3 EGGS SCRAMBLED

CUT THE TOP OF THE EGGPLANT OFF, PEEL THE SKIN OFF THE EGGPLANT AND CUP THE BOTTOM OFF **(JUST A LITTLE PIECE).** THINLY SLICE THE EGGPLANT IN THE ROUND AND PLACE THE PIECES ON A COOKY SHEET. SPRINKLE THE EGGPLANT ON BOTH SIDES WITH THE SALT AND LET SIT FOR ABOUT 30 MINUTES.

WHILE YOU ARE WAITING WISK THE EGGS IN A LARGE DISH. PUT THE BREAD CRUMBS IN A SEPARATE DISH ALSO.

NOW RINSE THE EGGPLANTS IN COLD WATER AND PAT DRY. HEAT UP THE VEGTABLE OIL IN A FRYING PAN. TAKE EACH PIECE OF EGGPLANT AND DIP IT FIRST IN EGG AND THEN IN BREAD CRUMBS COATING BOTH SIDES.

COOK IN FRYING PLAN ABOUT 3 MINUTES EACH SIDE AND THEN PLACE ON COOKY SHEET LINED WITH PAPER TOWEL TO DRAIN EXCESS OIL.

ARRANGE THE PIECES OF EGGPLANT ON A LARGE DISH. SPRINKLE WITH THE OLIVE OIL, CAPERS, BLACK PEPPER, BASIL AND SHAVED PARMASAN CHEESE.

PANSZANELLA

1 LOAF OF DAY OR TWO OLD HARD CRUSTED ITALIAN BREAD

2 LARGE FRESH TOMATOES

1 MEDIMUM RED ONION CUT IN HALF AND THEN CUT IN THIN STRIPS

½ CUP EXTRA VIRGIN OLIVE OIL

3 TABLESPOON FRESH BASIL

½ TEASPOON KOSHER OR SEA SALT

½ TEASPOON BLACK PEPPER

1 TABLESPOON BALSAMIC OR RED WINE VINEGAR

CUT UP ITALIAN BREAD INTO SMALL CUBES AND SOAK IN WARM WATER UNTIL SOFT. SQUEEZE THE WATER OUT OF THE BREAD AND PUT INTO A LARGE BOWL. CUT THE TOMATOES INTO ¼ INCH CUBES AND PLACE INTO THE BOWL. ADD THE RED THINLY SLICED ONION, ADD SALT AND PEPPER. RIPE THE BASIL INTO PIECES DO NOT CUT WITH A KNIFE. ADD THE OLIVE OIL AND VINEGAR, MIX TOGETHER. IF IT FEELS DRY ADD MORE OLIVE OIL.

THIS CAN BE SERVED AS AN APPETIZER OR WITH SHRIMP COCKTAIL OR ANYOTHER APPETIZER OF YOUR CHOSING.

DEEP FRIED CAULIFLOWERS

1 HEAD CAULIFLOWER CUT IN FLOWERETS

1 CUP FLOUR

½ TEASPOON KOSHER OR SEA SALT

½ TEASPOON BLACK PEPPER

½ CUP BACON **(CRISPY COOKED)**

½ CUP SQUASH AIOLI

¼ CUP HONEY

½ CUP PECANS

4 CUPS VEGTABLE OIL

HEAT UP THE OIL TO 350 DEGREES, TAKE TO CAULIFLOWERETS AND DREDGE IN FLOUR REMOVE THE EXCESS. PUT INTO HEATED OIL FOR ABOUT 3 MINUTES. REMOVE AND ADD THE REST OF INGREDIENTS IN A BOWL WITH THE CALIFLOWER AND MIX.

YOU CAN SUBSTITUTE BRUSSEL SPROUTS OR BROCCILI

RISOTTO BALLS

4 CUPS COOKED RICE **(WHITE OR ABORIO RICE)**

2 CUPS PARMESAN CHEESE

2 EGGS (SCRAMBLED)

½ TEASPOON KOSHER OR SEA SALT

½ TEASPOON WHITE PEPPER

MIX ALL INGREDIENTS TOGETHER AND ROLL INTO GOLF SIZE BALLS, THEN DEEP FRY IN 350 DEGREE VEGATABLE OIL OR CANOLA OIL UNTIL GOLDEN BROWN.

YOU CAN ALSO STUFF THE INSIDE OF THE BALL WITH ANYTHING YOU WANT. HAM, CHEESE OF YOU KIND, SUSAGE.

SERVE WITH MARINARA SAUCE, RECIPE IN THE COOKBOOK OR ANYOTHER SAUCE THAT YOU WANT.

GRAVLUX SALMON

2 CUPS KOSHER SALT

2 CUPS SUGAR

4 BUNCHES FENNEL FRONDS

1 PIECE OF SALMON **(ANY SALMON WILL DO)** REMOVE ALL BONES IF NEEDED

1 PLASTIC CONTAINER (**DO NOT USE A METAL CONTAINER)**

COMBINE BOTH THE SUGAR AND THE SALT IN A MIXING BOWL. TAKE THE PLASTIC CONTAINER AND TAKE 2 OF THE FENNEL FRONDS AND LAY THEM EVENLY IN THE BOTTOM OF THE CONTAINER. SPRKINKLE THE FENNEL WITH 2 CUPS OF THE COMBINED SALT & SUGAR. TAKE THE SALMON AND LAY IT SKIN SIDE DOWN ON THE SALT/SUGAR MIXTURE. PUT THE REMAINING FENNEL EVENLY ON TOP OF THE SALMON MEAT AND SPRINKLE THE REMAINING SUGAR/SALT ON TOP OF THE FENNEL.

COVER THE CONTAINER AND MAKE SURE THE AIR IS OUT OF THE CONTAINER & PUT IN THE REFRIGERATOR. SALMON WILL BE READY IN 4-6 HOURS.

REMOVE SALMON FROM CONTAINER, RINSE THROUGHLY IN COLD WATER PAT DRY AND WRAP IN PLASTIC WRAP. WHEN READY TO CUT, CUT THE SALMON ON AN ANGLE AS THIN AS YOU CAN.

CAN BE SERVED WITH TOAST, CRÈME FRIECH, SOUR CREAM, CAPERS AND FINELY CHOPPED RED ONIONS. EVEN SERVED ON PASTA.

STUFFED MUSHROOMS

6 OZS UNSALTED BUTTER

4 GARLIC CLOVES CHOPPED VERY FINELY

6 LARGE OPEN MUSHROOMS **(STEMS REMOVED) CHOP THE STEMS INTO SMALL PIECES**

2 OZS ITALIAN STYLE BREAD CRUMBS

1 TABLESPOON CHOPPED TYME

1 EGG BEATENED

½ TEASPOON KOSHER OR SEA SALT

½ TEASPOON BLACK PEPPER

PREHEAT OVEN TO 350 DEGREES. WHIP AND MELT THE BUTTER AND THE GARLIC TOGETHER. TAKE HALF THE MIXTURE AND RUB ALL THE SIDES OF THE MUSHROOMS AND PLACE ON A COOKING SHEET. OVER MEDUIM HEAT, COMBINE THE BREAD CRUMBS, PIECES OF THE STEMS, THE REST OF THE BUTTER AND GARLIC, THYME, SALT AND PEPPER AND BEATEN EGG IN A PAN. LET MISTURE COOL AND THEN STUFF EACH OF THE MUSHROOM CAPS. BAKE IN THE OVEN FOR 15 MINUTES OR UNTIL STUFFING IS GOLDEN BROWN. CAN BE SERVE HOT OR AT ROOM TEMPERATURE.

YOU CAN ADD ANY COOKED SEAFOOD, COOKED SUSAGE OR ANYTHING YOU DESIRE BEFORE PUTTING THEM IN THE OVEN.

SERVE THEM WITH ANY SAUCE YOU DESIRE FROM THIS COOKBOOK

CHILI SHRIMP

1 POUND RAW SHRIMP **(DESHELLED AND DEVAINED TAILS OFF)** ANY SIZE YOU DESIRE

1 SMALL RED CHILI OR RED CHILI POWDER

6 TABLESPOONS EXTRA VIRGIN OLIVE OIL

2 GARLIC CLOVES FINELY CHOPPED

½ KOSHER OR SEA SALT

½ TEASPOON BLACK PEPPER

1/8 TEASPOON PAPRIKA

ANY CRUSTY BREAD TO SERVE WITH THE SHRIMP **(FRENCH OR ITALIAN BREAD)**

IF YOU ARE USING THE CHILI PEPPER CUT THE PEPPER IN HALF LENGTHWISE, REMOVE THE SEEDS, AND FINELY CHOP THE FLESH. HEAT THE OIL IN A LARGE SKILLET OR CASSEROLE UNTIL THE OIL GETS VERY HOT. ADD THE GARLIC AND COOK FOR ABOUT 30 SECONDS THEN ADD THE SHRIMP, CHILI, PAPRIKA, SALT AND PEPPER AND COOK FOR 2-3 MINUTES CONSTANTLY STIRRING UNTIL THE SHRIMP TURN PINK.**(DO NOT OVER COOK THE SHRIMP STAY TO THE 3 MINUTE COOK TIME.)**

SERVE SHRIMP IN A DISH AND DRIZZLE WITH EXTRA VIRGIN OLIVE OIL. USE THE BREAD TO SOAK UP THE OIL.

SPICY SHRIMP IN SHERRY WINE

12 LARGE SHRIMP **(DESHELLED AND DEVAINED)** YOU CAN BUY THEM IN THE STORE LIKE THAT.

2 TABLESPOONS OLIVE OIL

4 TABLESPOONS DRY SHERRY WINE

¼ TEASPOON CAYENNE OR ¼ TEASPOON TABASCO SAUCE. **DEPENDING ON HOW HOT YOU WANT IT TO BE**

½ TEASPOON KOSHER OR SEA SALT

½ TEASPOON WHITE PEPPER

HEAT THE OIL IN A FRYING PAN. WHEN HOT ADD THE SHRIMP AND COOK OVER MEDIMUM HEAT STIRRING OCCASIONALLY FOR 2-3 MINUTES OR UNTIL THE SHRIMP TURN PINK. ADD THE SHERRY WINE, CAYENNE OR TABASCO SAUCE, SALT AND PEPPER. SERVE ON A SERVING PLATE WITH TOOTHPICKS OR SMALL FINGER FORKS.

EGGPLANT DIP

1 LARGE EGGPLANT

6 TABLESPOONS OLIVE OIL

3 SCALLIONS FINELY CHOPPED

1 LARGE GARLIC CLOVE FINELY CHOPPED

2 TABLESPOONS PARSLEY CHOPPED FINE **(NO STEMS)**

1/8 TEASPOON SMOKED SWEET PAPRIKA

½ TEASPOON KOSHER OR SEA SALT

½ TEASPOON WHITE PEPPER

PEEL THE SKIN OFF THE EGGPLANT AND THEN CUT IN LONG STRIPS. SPRINKLE THE EGGPLANT ON BOTH SIDES WITH THE SALT AND LET STAND FOR 30 MINUTES TO REMOVE THE BITTERNESS. RINSE THE EGGPLANT IN COLD WATER TO REMOVE THE SALT AND LIQUID. PUT 3 TABLESPOONS OF THE OLIVE OIL IN A SKILLET AND HEAT. PUT THE EGGPLANT IN THE SKILLET AND COOK BOTH SIDES UNTIL BOTH SIDES ARE BROWN. REMOVE EGGPLANT AND PUT ON PAPER TOWELS TO DRAIN OFF THE OIL. ADD THE REMAINING OIL TO A FRYING PAN AND ADD THE SCALLIONS AND GARLIC AND COOK FOR 3 MINUTES UNTIL THE SCALLIONS ARE SOFT. REMOVE FROM HEAT AND LET COOL WITH THE EGGPLANT. PUT ALL THE INGREDIENTS IN THE FOOD PROCESSOR AND PROCESS UNTIL CHUNCKY. STIR IN THE PARSLEY, AND TASTE, ADD SALT AND PEPPER TO TASTE.

SERVE WITH EITHER FRENCH OR ITALIAN CRUSTY BREAD.

ASPARAGUS ROASTED WITH PROSCIUTTO ITALIAN HAM

2 TEASPOONS EXTRA VIRGIN OLIVE OIL

6 SLICES OF PROSCIUTTO HAM

12 ASPARAGUS SPEARS

½ TEASPOON WHITE PEPPER

PREPARING THE ASPARAGUS: TAKE EACH ASPARAGUS AND BEND EACH ONE. IT WILL BREAK AT THE WOODY END. PUT THE ASPARAGUS IN A BOWL AND DRIZZLE WITH OLIVE OIL MAKE SURE EACH ONE IS COATED WELL.

PREHEAT OVEN TO 400 DEGREES, TAKE A SLICE OF PROSCIUTTO AND WRAP EACH ASPARAGUS SPEAR. PLACE ON IN A ROASTING PAN THAT HAS BEEN COATED WITH OLIVE OIL. COOK FOR ABOUT 10 MINUTES, DEPENDING ON SIZE BUT MAKING SURE NOT TO OVERCOOK. BE SURE THEY ARE STILL FIRM AND YOU ARE ABLE TO HANDLE.

SERVE HOT OR AT ROOM TEMPERATURE. THERE ARE MANY SAUCES THAT YOU CAN SERVE AS A DIP FOR THESE; YOUR CHOICE IS IN THIS COOKBOOK.

IF YOU CANNOT FIND PROSCIUTTO HAM, ANY THINLY SLICED DELI HAM WILL DO.

COOKED SHRIMP IN LIME

ZEST AND JUICE OF 6 LIMES

12 RAW SHRIMP **(DESHELLED AND DEVAINED) (LEAVE TAIL ON)**

4 TABLESPOONS OLIVE OIL

2 GARLIC CLOVES FINELY CHOPPED

3 TABLESPOONS SHERRY WINE

½ TEASPOON KOSHER OR SEA SALT

½ TEASPOON WHITE PEPPER

4 TABLESPOONS FLAT LEAF PARSLEY CHOPPED FINELY **(NO STEMS)**

IN A DEEP FRYING PAN ADD ½ THE OLIVE OIL AND THE GARLIC, COOK FOR ABOUT 30 SECONDS AND THEN ADD THE SHRIMP. COOK THE SHRIMP FOR ABOUT 3-4 MINUTES ADDING THE SALT AND PEPPER, ZEST AND JUICE OF THE LIMES AND THE SHERRY. COOK UNTIL THEY TURN PINK. **(DO NOT OVERCOOK).** PLACE IN A DISH AND ADD THE REMAINING OLIVE OIL, AND THE PARSLEY.

OLIVES WITH ORANGE PEEL, ORANGE JUICE, OLIVE OIL AND LEMON PEEL AND JUICE

3 CUPS OF OLIVES **(ANY OLIVES WILL DO TRY A MIXTURE)**

2 ORANGES, ORANGE ZEST AND JUICE

1 LEMON ZEST AND JUICE

1 TABLESPOON FINELY CHOPPED GARLIC

1/8 TEASPOON KOSHER OR SEA SALT

¼ TEASPOON BLACK PEPPER

¼ TEASPOON CRUSHED RED PEPPER FLAKES- **(MORE OR LESS IF YOU DESIRE)**

½ CUP EXTRA VIRGIN OLIVE OIL

PUT THE OLIVES IN A SERVING DISH. IN A SAUCE PAN, ADD THE OLIVE OIL, GARLIC, SALT AND PEPPER AND CRUSH RED PEPPER FLAKES. PUT ON LOW HEAT; DO NOT BRING TO BOIL JUST WARM THE INGREDIENTS UP. PUT THE ZEST AND THE JUICES OF BOTH ORANGES AND LEMON IN THE BOWL. COVER THE OLIVES WITH THE OIL AND MIX. LET SIT FOR ABOUT 1 HOUR TO SOAK UP THE OIL AND JUICES.

SERVE WITH CRUSTY BREAD AND TOOTHPICKS.

ROASTED RED BELL PEPPERS

4 RED BELL PEPPERS

4 TABLESPOONS FINELY CRUSHED GARLIC

½ TABLESPOON KOSHER OR SEA SALT

½ TABLESPOON WHITE PEPPER

1 TABLESPOON OREGANO

½ CUP EXTRA VIRGIN OLIVE OIL

2 TABLESPOONS PARSLEY FINELY CHOPPED **(NO STEMS)**

THERE ARE TWO DIFFERENT WAYS TO ROAST RED PEPPERS.

1. CUT PEPPERS IN HALF REMOVE THE SEEDS AND CORE, RUB WITH OLIVE OIL AND PUT IN A 450 DEGREE OVEN UNTIL THE SKIN IS CHARED. REMOVE THE PEPPERS AND PUT IN A BOWL AND WRAP THE OUTSIDE OF THE BOWL WITH SARAN WRAP AND SET ASIDE. REMOVE THE WRAP AND PEEL THE SKIN OFF THE PEPPERS. **DO NOT WASH THE PEPPERS UNDER WATER.**

2. RUB THE OUTSIDE OF THE PEPPERS AND PUT ON THE OUTSIDE GRILL ON HIGH HEAT. TURN THE PEPPERS ON ALL SIDES AND REMOVE THE PEPPERS WHEN THE SKIN IS BLACK CHARED. PUT THEM IN A BOWL AND WRAP THE BOWL WITH SARAN WRAP. NOW UNWRAP AFTER ABOUT 1 HOUR, PEEL THE SKIN OFF AND REMOVE THE CORE AND THE SEEDS FROM INSIDE OF THE PEPPER. **DO NOT WASH THE PEPPERS UNDER WATER.**

YOU CAN SERVE THESE TWO WAYS:

1. COMBINE ALL INGREDIENTS IN A BLENDER AND SERVE AS A DIP OR A SAUCE ON MEATS, SEAFOOD, AND POULTRY.

2 ARRANGE THE PEPPERS IN A DISH AND ADD THE REST OF THE INGREDIENTS ON TOP OF THE PEPPERS.

ROASTED RED BELL PEPPER AND EGGPLANT DIP

4 RED BELL PEPPERS

4 TABLESPOONS FINELY CRUSHED GARLIC

½ TABLESPOON KOSHER OR SEA SALT

½ TABLESPOON WHITE PEPPER

1 TABLESPOON ORGANEO

½ CUP EXTRA VIRGIL OLIVE OIL

2 TABLESPOONS PARSLEY FINELY CHOPPED **(NO STEMS)**

THERE ARE TWO DIFFERENT WAYS TO ROAST RED PEPPERS.

1. CUT PEPPERS IN HALF REMOVE THE SEEDS AND CORE, RUB WITH OLIVE OIL AND PUT IN A 450 DEGREE OVEN UNTIL THE SKIN IS CHARED. REMOVE THE PEPPERS AND PUT IN A BOWL AND WRAP THE OUTSIDE OF THE BOWL WITH SARAN WRAP AND SET ASIDE. REMOVE THE WRAP AND PEEL THE SKIN OFF THE PEPPERS. **DO NOT WASH THE PEPPERS UNDER WATER.**

YOU CAN SERVE THESE TWO WAYS:

1. COMBINE ALL INGREDIENTS IN A BLENDER AND SERVE AS A DIP OR A SAUCE ON MEATS, SEAFOOD, AND POULTRY.

2 ARRANGE THE PEPPERS IN A DISH AND ADD THE REST OF THE INGREDIENTS ON TOP OF THE PEPPERS.

FOR THE EGGPLANT FOLLOW THE RECIPE FOR EGGPLANT ON PAGE 21, AND THEN COMBINE EACH ONE IN THE FOOD PROCESSOR AND LEAVES CHUNCKY

LARGE GARLIC SHRIMP

12 LARGE SHRIMP (DESHELLED AND DEVEINED **(LEAVE TAILS ON)**

5 CLOVES GARLIC FINELY CHOPPED

½ TEASPOONS KOSHER OR SEA SALT

½ TEASPOONS WHITE PEPPER

1 TEASPOON RED PEPPER FLAKES

6 TABLESPOONS EXTRA VIRGIN OLIVE OIL

2 TABLESPOON SHERRY VINEGAR

2 TABLESPOONS CHOPPED PARSLEY **(NO STEMS)**

IN A FRYING PAN ADD HALF THE OIL AND HEAT ON MEDIMUM HIGH HEAT. ADD THE SHRIMP AND COOK FOR 3 MINUTS, TURN AFTER 3 MINUTES. WHEN YOU TURN THEM ADD THE GARLIC, SALT, PEPPER, RED PEPPER FLAKES AND THE SHERRY VINEGAR. REMOVE FROM HEAT, PUT ON A PLATER AND ADD THE REST OF THE INGREDIENTS. SERVE BY THEMSELVES OR ADD OVER PASTA.

SHRIMP COCKTAIL

12 LARGE SHRIMP **(PEELED AND DEVAINED)** LEAVE TAIL ON.

JUICE AND ZEST OF 2 LEMONS OR LIMES **(YOUR CHOICE)**

2 TABLESPOONS KOSHER OR SEA SALT

IN A LARGE DEEP POT PUT ABOUT 6 CUPS OF COLD WATER. BRING WATER TO A BOIL AND ADD THE SALT, LEMON OR LIME JUICE AND ZEST AND THE SHRIMP. WHEN WATER COMES BACK TO A BOIL COOK FOR 3 MINUTES ONLY. DRAIN THE WATER AND COOL THE SHRIMP UNDER COLD WATER TO STOP THE COOKING. DRAIN THE WATER AND PUT SHRIMP IN REFRIGERATOR UNTIL READY TO SERVE COVERED WITH PLASTIC WRAP.

FOLLOW THE RECEIPE FOR THE BLOODY MARY COCKTAIL SAUCE ON PAGE 53 IN THIS COOKBOOK.

SERVE IN ANY SINGLE DISH OF YOUR CHOSING WITH THE COCKTAIL SAUCE.

YOUR CAN ALSO CHOSE ANY DRESSING OR SAUCE FROM THIS COOKBOOK SHOULD YOU DESIRE OR SERVE DIFFERENT ONES.

BAKED SCALLOPS

1 LB OF DIVER OR BABY SCALLOPS **(IF DIVER TYPE, CUT IN QUARTERS, IF BABY SCALLOPS LEAVE THEM HOLE)**

2 REGULAR SIZE ONIONS FINELY CHOPPED **(ANY ONION WILL DO)**

2 GARLIC CLOVES FINELY CHOPPED

3 TABLESPOONS TARRAGON FINELY CHOPPED

1/8 TEASPOON NUTMEG

1/8 TEASPOON GROUND CLOVE

2 TABLESPOONS OLIVE OIL

¼ TEASPOON KOSHER OR SEA SALT

¼ TEASPOON WHITE PEPPER

2 TABLESPOONS FRESH WHITE BREAD CRUMBS

4 SMALL RAMEKINS OR 4 SCALLOP SHELLS

PREHEAT OVEN TO 400 DEGREES. MIX THE SCALLOPS, ONIONS, GARLIC, 2 TABLESPOONS OF TARRAGON, THE NUTMEG AND THE CLOVE IN A LARGE BOWL WITH THE SALT AND PEPPER.

IN OVEN PROOF DISHES OR SCALLOP SHELLS, DIVIDE THE MIXTURE AMONG CONTAINERS. SPRINKLE THE TOP OF EACH WITH THE BREAD CRUMBS, OLIVE OIL AND THE REST OF THE TARRAGON.

BAKE IN THE PREHEATED OVEN FOR 15 – 20 MINUTES OR UNTIL GOLDEN BROWN.

YOU CAN SUBSTITUTE LOBSTER, CRAB OR SHRIMP

CHICKEN LIVERS IN MARINARA SAUCE

1 LB CHICKEN LIVERS

2 TABLESPOONS EXTRA VIRGIN OLIVE OIL

1 SMALL YELLOW OR RED ONION CHOPPED VERY FINE

2 GARLIC CLOVES PEELED AND CHOPPED VERY FINE

3 ½ OZS SHERRY WINE

¼ TEASPOON KOSHER OR SEA SALT

¼ TEASPOON WHITE PEPPER

3 TABLESPOON CHOPPED FLAT LEAF PARSLEY

CRUSTY BREAD **(ANY BREAD WILL DO)**

MAKE SURE YOU TRIM THE LIVERS CUTTING AWAY THE DUCTS AND GRISTLES. THEN CUT INTO SMALL PIECES, **(BITE SIZE)**. HEAT THE OLIVE OIL INTO A HEAVY SKILLET ADD THE ONION AND COOK FOR 5 MINUTES UNTIL SOFT BUT NOT BROWN. ADD THE GARLIC AND COOK FOR 30 SECONDS MORE.

ADD THE CHICKEN LIVERS TO THE SKILLET AND COOK FOR 2-3 MINUTES, STIRRING ALL THE TIME UNTIL THE LIVERS TURN COLOR AND ARE FIRM BUT ARE STILL PINK INSIDE. ADD THE SHERRY WINE AND REDUCE BY HALF. THEN ADD THE MARINARA SAUCE AND COOK FOR ANOTHER 7 -8 MINUTES ON A LOW BOIL.

MARINARA RECEIPE IN COOK BOOK ON PAGE 51.

SERVE IN A DISH AND ADD THE PARSLEY AND SERVE WITH THE BREAD.

CAN ALSO BE SERVED OVER ANY PASTA.

DRESSINGS

BASIL/BUTTERMILK DRESSING

1 CUP BUTTERMILK

½ CUP MAYO

½ CUP BASIL LEAVES **(NO STEMS)**

4 CLOVES GARLIC

½ TABLESPOON WHITE VINEGAR

½ TEASPOON KOSHER OR SEA SALT

½ TEASPOON WHITE PEPPER

COMBINE ALL INGREDIENTS IN FOOD PROCESSOR AND BLEND UNTIL SMOOTH.

CAN BE USED ON ANY SALAD THAT YOU WANT TO MAKE.

BASIL AIOLI DRESSING

1 CUP MAYO

1 CUP BASIL LEAVES ONLY **(NO STEMS)**

1 TSP CHOPPED GARLIC

JUICE AND ZEST OF 1 LEMON

1 ANCHOVY

PUT INGREDIENTS IN BLENDER AND BLEND UNTIL SMOOTH. REFRIGERATE IMMEDIATELY AFTER BLENDING TO HOLD COLOR. **TO SERVE** REMOVE FROM REFRIGERATOR AND LET STAND AT ROOM TEMPERATURE FOR 15 MINUTES

CAN BE USED AS A SALAD DRESSING OR ON TOP OF MEATS AND FISH

APPLE AIOLI DRESSING

1 CUP MAYO

1 APPLE CORDED, PEELED AND DICED

JUICE OF 1 LEMON

1 TEASPOON OF DIJON MUSTARD

1 TEASPOON OF BROWN SUGAR

¼ CUP SHERRY VINEGAR

PUREE ALL INGREDIENTS IN BLENDER UNTIL SMOOTH AND CREAMY.

SERVE THIS ON TOP OF A BEET OR APPLE SALAD OR WITH YOUR FAVORITE SALAD

CHERRY TOMATO SAUCE DRESSING

2 PINTS OF CHERRY TOMATOES

½ TABLESPOON KOSHER OR SEA SALT

½ TABLESPOON BLACK PEPPER

1 TEASPOON RED PEPPER FLAKES

1 TABLESPOON ROASTED GARLIC

1 AHCHOVY

½ TABLESPOON OREGANO

½ CUP OLIVE OIL

TOSS CHERRY TOMATOES WITH OLIVE OIL, SALT, PEPPER & ORGANO IN A LARGE BOWL AND SPREAD OUT ON COOKIE SHEET AND BAKE FOR 10-12 MINUTES AT 400 DEGREES.

PUT ALL INGREDIENTS IN FOOD PROCESSOR AND BLEND. LEAVE CHUNKY

SERVE ON ANY PASTA THAT YOU WANT

CHIMICHURRI SAUCE

½ TEASPOON RED PEPPER FLAKES

1 TABLESPOON GARLIC PUREE

½ CUP OREGANO FRESH LEAVES

1 CUP PARSLEY LEAVES

6 THINLY SLICED DILL PICKLES

JUICE AND ZEST OF 1 LEMON

½ TEASPOON KOSHER SALT

½ TEASPOON WHITE PEPPER

½ CUP OLIVE OIL

PUT IN FOOD PROCESSOR- **LEAVE CHUNKY**

SERVE AS A CONDIMENT FOR PORK OR VEAL DISHES.

FRENCH DRESSING

1/2 CUP SUGAR

1/2 CUP OLIVE OIL

1/2 CUP VINGAR

1/2 CAN TOMATO SOUP

1/8 TEASPOON WHITE PEPPER

1/2 TEASPOON KOSHER OR SEA SALT

1/2 TEASPOON GARLIC POWDER

1/2 TEASPOON PAPRIKA

1/2 TEASPOON OREGANO

1/2 TEASPOON A-1 STEAK SAUCE

1/2 TEASPOON WORSTERSHERE

COMBINE ALL INGREDIENTS IN BLENDER UNITL SMOOTH.

USE ON ANY SALAD MIXTURE WETHER IT BE LETTUCES OR BEETS OR FRUIT SALADS.

CITRUS VINEGARETTE

JUICE AND ZEST OF 1 LEMON- 1 ORANGE & 2 LIMES

1 CUP OF EXTRA VIRGIN OLIVE OIL

1 TABLESPOON SUGAR

½ TABLESPOON KOSHER OR SEA SALT

MIX ALL INGREDIENTS IN A BOWL WITH A WISK.

CAN BE PUT ON ANY TYPE OF GREENS OR FRUIT SALAD WITH GREENS.

COGNAC MAYO DRESSING

¾ CUP MAYO

1 TABLESPOON GARLIC **(FINELY CHOPPED)**

3 TABLESPOONS PARMESAN CHEESE

1 TABLESPOON LEMON JUICE

2 TABLESPOONS COGNAC

COMBINE ALL INGREDIENTS IN A BOWL AND WISK UNTIL BLENDED.

CAN BE USED TO TOP THE OYSTERS WHEN MAKING OYSTERS ROCKERFELLER, BAKED CLAMS, STUFF LOBSTERS, AND CAN BE PUT ON TOP OF ANY FISH WHEN SERVING.

LOBSTER/SHRIMP POOR BOY DRESSING

1 CUP MAYO

JUICE OF 1 LEMON

3 TABLESPOONS GRAINY MUSTARD

1 TABLESPOONS SIRRACHA

½ RED ONION CHOPPED FINELY

1 TABLESPOON DILL CHOPPED FINE

COMBINES ALL INGREDIENTS IN BLENDER UNTIL SMOOTH.

CAN BE SERVED ON ANY SEAFOOD SANDWICH OR SEAFOOD COCKTAIL.

MUSTARD MARMALADE

½ CUP ROASTED GARLIC

3 SHALLOTS SLICED VERY THIN

½ CUP RED WINE VINEGAR

½ CUP WATER

1 CUBE OF BEEF STOCK

2 TABLESPOONS BROWN SUGAR

½ CUP MAYO

1 TABLESPOON DIJON MUSTARD

COOK THE FIRST 6 ITEMS IN SAUCE PAN FOR 45 MINUTES. LET COOL FOR AN HOUR. PUT IN BLENDER AND PUREE WITH 1/2 CUP OF MAYO AND 1 TABLESPOON OF DIJON MUSTARD.

SERVE WITH SHRIMP, CRAB OR LOBSTER COCKTAIL. OR AS A MAIN DISH.

GARLIC AIOLI

3 BULBS GARLIC

1/8 TEASPOON KOSHER OR SEA SALT

1/8 TEASPOON WHITE PEPPER

3 TABLESPOONS OLIVE OIL

½ CUP CHICKEN STOCK

1 TABLESPOON HEAVY CREAM

CUT THE TOPS OFF OF THE GARLIC BULBS. PUT EACH ONE ON A PIECE OF ALUMIUM FOIL. DRIZZLE EACH BULB WITH OIL AND SPRINKLE WITH SALT AND PEPPER. WRAP EACH, PUT ON A COOKIE SHEET AND PLACE IN THE OVEN AT 350 DEGRESS FOR ABOUT 25-30 MINUTES OR UNTIL GARLIC IS SOFT TO THE TOUCH THROUGH THE FOIL.

LET COOL AND SQUEEZE THE CLOVES OUT OF THE SKIN INTO A FOOD PROCESSOR. AND ADD THE REMAINING INGREDIENTS AND PROCESS UNTIL SMOOTH.

CUCUMBER MIGNONETTE

1 CUP RICE WINE VINEGAR

1 SHALLOT **(FINELY CHOPPED)**

1 INCH PIECE OF GINGER **(MINCED VERY FINELY)**

½ CUCUMBER PEELED, SEEDED, AND MINCED FINELY

1 TABLESPOON SUGAR

½ TEASPOON BLACK PEPPER

COMBINE ALL INGREDIENTS BY HAND, CAN BE USED ON RAW OYSTERS, COOKED SHRIMP, COOKED SCALLOPS. AS A DIPPING SAUCE.

GARLIC HORSERADISH PUREE

4 WHOLE BULBS OF GARLIC

½ CUP CHICKEN STOCK

1 ½ TABLESPOONS HORSERADISH

2 TABLESPOONS HEAVY CREAM

¼ TEASPOON KOSHER OR SEA SALT

¼ TEASPOON WHITE PEPPER

4 TABLESPOONS OLIVE OIL

CUT THE TOPS OF THE GARLIC BULBS OFF AND RUB WITH OLIVE OIL AND WRAP EACH ON IN ALUMIUM FOIL. PLACE ON COOKIE SHEET AND BAKE IN OVEN AT 350 DEGREES FOR ABOUT 25-30 MINUTES OR UNTIL THE BULBS ARE SOFT TO THE TOUCH.

REMOVE THE GARLIC FROM THE SKIN BY SQUEEZING THE BULBS BE CAREFUL NOT TO GET ANY SKIN IN THE FOOD PROCESSOR. ADD THE REST OF THE INGREDIENTS IN FOOD PPROCESSOR AND BLEND UNTIL SMOOTH.

CAN BE USED TO DRESS ANY SALAD, MEATS OR SEAFOODS.

SALSA VERDE

1 CUP PARSLEY **(LEAVES ONLY NO STEMS)**

2 TEASPOONS CAPERS

½ CUP OLIVE OIL

2 ANCHOVIES

JUICE AND ZEST OF 1 LEMON

2 TABLESPOONS ROASTED GARLIC

2 TABLESPOON DIJON MUSTARD

¼ TEASPOON WHITE PEPPER

BLEND ALL INGREDIENTS IN FOOD PROCESSOR UNTIL CHUNCKY.

CAN BE USED AS A SEAFOOD DIP, SERVE ON TOP OF PORK, STEAKS OR ANYOTHER MEATS.

ROASTED GARLIC PUREE

4 GARLIC BULBS

½ CUP CHICKEN STOCK

¼ TEASPOON KOSHER OR SEA SALT

¼ TEASPOON WHITE PEPPER

4 TABLESPOONS OLIVE OIL

CUT THE TOP OF EACH GARLIC BULB AND PLACE ON SEPARATE SHEETS OF ALUMIUM. DRIZZLE EACH BULB WITH THE OLIVE OIL, SALT AND PEPPER, WRAP AND PLACE ON COOKIE SHEET. ROAST IN OVEN AT 350 DEGREES FOR ABOUT 20-30 MINUTES OR UNTIL THE BULBS ARE SOFT TO THE TOUCH.

LET THE BULBS COOL, AND THEN SQUEEZE EACH BULB TO REMOVE THE GARLIC IN THE BLENDER, BUT BE CAREFUL NOT TO GET ANY SKIN IN THE BLENDER. ADD THE REST OF THE INGREDIENTS AND BLEND UNTIL SMOOTH. STORE IN REFRIGERATOR.

CAN BE MIXED WITH MASH POTATOES, SPREAD ON TOAST, AND EVEN ON PRETTY MUCH ANYTHING YOU LIKE WITH GARLIC.

SAFFRON DRESSING

1 TEASPOON SAFFRON THREADS

2 TABLESPOONS HOT WATER

5 OZ MAYO

2 TABLESPOON GRATED ONION

4 TABLESPOONS LEMON JUICE

1 TEASPOONS DIJON MUSTARD

HEAT THE SAFFRON THREADS IN THE HOT WATER. REMOVE FROM HEAT AND LET COOL. WHEN COOL MIX IN THE REMAINDER OF THE INGREDIENTS.

CAN BE USED ON COOKED SHRIMP, COOKED SCALLOPS OR ANY FISH. ALSO AS AND APPETIZER OR FOR A MAIN MEAL DRESSING.

HONEY MUSTARD BACON AIOLI

2 TABLESPOONS DIJON MUSTARD

2 TABLESPOONS HONEY

2 TABLESPOONS BACON FAT

2 CUPS MAYO

COMBINE ALL INGREDIENTS IN BLENDER AND BLEND UNTIL SMOOTH. CAN BE SERVED ON ANY SALAD.

ORANGE JULIUS DRESSING

½ QUART PURE ORANGE JUICE

¼ QUART HEAVY CREAM

1/8 CUP HONEY

1/8 CUP WHITE VINAGAR

1 TEASPOON PURE VANILLA EXTRACT

PUT ALL INGREDIENTS IN A POT AND COOK TILL REDUCED BY HALF. CAN BE USED AS A SALAD DRESSING FOR ANY FRUIT SALAD OR A MIXTURE OF GREENS AND FRUIT SALAD.

ROASTED GARLIC DRESSING

1 ½ CUPS BUTTERMILK

2 CUPS MAYO

½ CUP GRATED PARMASAN CHEESE

JUICE AND ZEST OF 1 LEMON

1 ANCHOVY

2 TEASPOONS WHITE PEPPER

1 TABLESPOON BALSAMIC VINEGAR

4 TABLESPOONS ROASTED GARLIC PUREE (RECEIPE ON PAGE 31)

COMBINE ALL INGREDIENTS IN BLENDER UNTIL SMOOTH.

USE AS SALAD DRESSING, DIPPING SAUCE FOR SEAFOOD, VEGATABLE DIP.

SAUCES

MARINARA SAUCE

1 ONION SMALL DICE FINE

2 TABLESPOONS MINCED GARLIC

1 ANCHOVY

1 CUP OLIVE OIL

1 ½ CUPS BASIL (**NO STEMS)** CHOPPED

1 (10 OZ) CAN PLUM TOMATOES

¼ TEASPOON CRUSH RED PEPPER FLAKES **OR MORE IF DESIRED**

¼ TEASPONN KOSHER OR SEA SALT

¼ TEASPOON BLACK PEPPER

½ CUP RED WINES (**NOT COOKING WINE)**

COMBINE ALL INGREDIENTS EXCEPT THE BASIL AND PLUM TOMATOES IN A SAUCE PAN. SWEAT INGREDIENTS UNTIL TRANSLUCENT AND ANCHOVY UNTIL IT HAS DISSOLVED. ADD PLUM TOMATOES AND BASIL AND SIMMER FOR 45 MINUTES ON MEDIUM HEAT. USE POTATO MASHER TO BREAKDOWN TOMATOES DOWN OR BLEND IT SMOOTH IF YOU DESIRE.

TOMATO FENNEL SAUCE

3 TABLESPOONS UNSALTED BUTTER

½ FENNEL BULB CUT IN QUARTERS

½ SWEET ONION PEELED AND CUT IN QUARTERS

5 GARLIC CLOVES PEELED

2 STALKS CELERY CHOPPED

1 JALEPENO SEEDED THEN CUT IN SMALL PIECES

½ TEASPOON KOSHER OR SEA SALT

½ TEASPOON WHITE PEPPER

½ CUP WHITE WINE

1 BOTTLE CLAM JUICE

(1) 15 OZ CAN OF PLUM TOMATOES

TAKE THE CAN OF PLUM TOMATOES AND BLEND IN A BLENDER UNTIL SMOOTH AND SET ASIDE. IN A LARGE SAUCE PAN MELT THE BUTTER THEN ADD THE CUT FENNEL, JALEPENO, ONION, GARLIC, CELERY, SALT AND PEPPER. COOK UNTIL EVERYTHING IS SOFT BUT NOT BROWN. ADD THE WINE AND CLAM JUICE AND REDUCE BY HALF. NOW ADD THE BLENDED TOMATOES AND COOK FOR ABOUT 15 TO 20 MINUTES. REMOVE FROM HEAT AND STRAIN AND STORE IN REFRIGERATOR.

BLOODY MARY SAUCE

½ CUP KETCHUP

1 RIPE TOMATO

1 CELERY STALK COARSELY CHOPPED

½ ONION COURSELY CHOPPED

2 TABLESPOONS HORSERADISH

JUICE OF 1 LEMON

2 TEASPOONS TABASCO SAUCE

1 TABLESPOON WORCESTERSHIRE SAUCE

1 OZ VODKA **(NONE FLAVORED)**

1 TEASPOON CELERY SEED SPICE

½ TEASPOON KOSHER OR SEA SALT

½ TEASPOON WHITE PEPPER

COMBINE ALL INGREDIIENTS IN FOOD PROCESSOR AND LEAVE CHUNKY

SERVE WITH SHRIMP, CRAB OR LOBSTER OR ANY OTHER SEAFOOD AS A COCKTAIL SAUCE.

RASBERRY/MUSTARD SAUCE

1 CAN RED RASPBERRIES

2 TABLESPOONS DIJON MUSTARD

2 TABLESPOONS SUGAR

½ TEASPOON EXTRA VIRGIN OLIVE OIL

½ TEASPOON SHERRY VINEGAR

PUT INGREDIENTS IN BLENDER AND BLEND FOR 1 ½ MINUTES. STORE IN REFRIGERATOR.

SERVE ON TOP OF PORK DISHES, VEAL DISHES, EVEN SEAFOOD

RED WINE SAUCE

3 CUPS OF ANY RED WINE (**DO NOT USE ANY COOKING WINES)**

1 (12OZ JAR) OF SAVORY BEEF OR HOME MADE BEEF STOCK

1/8 TEASPOON SUGAR

1/8 TEASPOON KOSHER OR SEA SALT

1/8 TEASPOON WHITE PEPPER

PUT ALL INGREDIENTS IN A SAUCE PAN OVER MEDIUM HEAT AND REDUCE BY HALF.

CAN BE SERVE OVER ANY MEAT, CHICKEN, SEAFOOD, VEAL OR LAMB

PORT WINE SAUCE

2 CUPS ANY PORT WINE

¼ CUP SUGAR

1/8 TEASPOON KOSHER OR SEA SALT

1/8 TEASPOON WHITE PEPPER

PUT ALL INGREDIENTS IN A SAUCE PAN AND PUT ON MEDIMUM HEAT AND REDUCE BY HALF

CAN BE USED AS A SAUCE FOR ANY MEAT OR SEAFOOD.

PEAR VINGARETTE SAUCE

JUICE 2 PEARS AND PUT ON STOVE ON MEDIUM HEAT. REDUCE BY HALF **OR USE 1 CAN OF PEAR JUICE**

THEN REMOVE FROM STOVE AND COMBINE WITH THE REMAINING INGREDIENTS

2 OZS OF CHAMPAGNE VINGAR

6 OZS OF OLIVE OIL

1 MINCED SHALLOT

1 TEASPOON HONEY

¼ TEASPOONS KOSHER OR SEA SALT

¼ TEASPOON WHITE PEPPER

PUT ALL INGREDIENTS IN BLENDER AND BLEND UNTIL SMOOTH.

CAN BE SERVED WITH ANY TYPE OF GREENS OR BEET SALAD.

LEMON BASIL BUTTER SAUCE

ZEST AND JUICE OF 2 LEMONS

4 ROASTED GARLIC CLOVES MASHED

½ CUP BASIL LEAVES CHOPPED FINE. (NO STEMS)

2 CUPS OLIVE OIL

¼ CUP UNSALTED BUTTER

¼ CUP CAPERS

¼ CUP WHITE WINE **(DO NOT USE COOKING WINE)**

PUT ALL INGREDIENTS IN A SAUCE PAN ON MEDIUM HEAT UNTIL BUTTER IS MELTED AND THE INGREDIENTS ARE WARM TO THE TASTE. KEEP WARM OVER LOW HEAT UNTIL YOU USE IT.

(DO NOT BRING TO A BOIL)

WASABI CRÈME FRAICHE

1/3 CUP WASABI POWDER-**(EQUAL AMOUNTS OF WATER AND WASABI) OR 2 TABLESPOONS WASABI PASTE.**

1/2 CUP MAYO

1/2 CUP CRÈME FRAICHE

1/2 TABLESPOON SALT

½ CUP BASIL LEAVES **(JUST LEAVES NO STEMS)**

PUREE IN BLENDER UNTIL SMOOTH

CAN BE SERVED ON FISH, MEAT, PORK, CHICKEN OR VEAL. OR WHEREVER YOU LIKE.

SMOKED SALMON SAUCE

1 ½ CUPS CHOPPED SHALLOTS

¼ CUP BUTTER

COMBINE BOTH INGREDIENTS AND SIMMER UNTIL SHALLOTS ARE SOFT. WHEN SOFT

PUT IN BLENDER AND ADD THE FOLLOWING INGREDIENTS:

2 OUNCES PLAIN VODKA

¼ CUP GORGONZOLA CHEESE

1 CUP HEAVY CREAM

½ CUP BASIL LEAVES **(NO STEMS)**

½ TEASPOON KOSHER OR SEA SALT

4 OUNCES SMOKED SALMON

COMBINE ALL INGREDIENTS IN FOOD PROCESSOR UNTIL SMOOTH. STORE IN REFRIGERATOR.

SERVE AS A TOPPING FOR THE SALMON, USE ALSO FOR CRAB, LOBSTER OR SEAFOOD SALAD

BERNAISE SAUCE

3 EGG YOLKS

½ LB UNSLATED SWEET MELTED BUTTER

JUICE OF ONE LEMON

2 TABLESPOONS CHOPPED FINE TARRAGON

1/8 TEASPOON KOSHER OR SEA SALT

1/8 TEASPOON WHITE PEPPER

WHIP EGG YOLKS UNTIL CREAMY THEN SLOWLY ADD MELTED BUTTER AND JUICE OF LEMON AND TARRAGON. MIX ALL INGREDIENTS OVER VERY LOW HEAT. **DO NOT BRING TO A BOIL**. WHEN ALL INGREDIENTS ARE MIXED TOGETHER REMOVE FROM HEAT AND KEEP WARM IN A THERMOS OR DOUBLE BOILER.

IF REFRIGERATED BRING BACK TO HEAT ON A VERY LOW HEAT.

CAN BE SERVED ON TOP OF ANY MEAT, SEAFOOD, CHICKEN, OR DUCK.

WHITE WINE SAUCE

2 CLOVES PEELED GARLIC **(CHOPPED VERY FINELY)**

1 TABLESPOON CAPERS

JUICE OF 1 LEMON

¼ TEASPOON KOSHER OR SEA SALT

¼ TEASPOON WHITE PEPPER

4 TABLESPOONS OLIVE OIL

4 TABLESPOONS UNSALTED BUTTER

½ CUP WHITE WINE **(NOT COOKING WINE)** ANY WHITE WINE THAT YOU DRINK

IN A SAUCE PAN ADD THE OLIVE OIL AND HEAT ON MEDIMUM HIGH HEAT. ADD THE GARLIC, CAPERS, SALT AND PEPPER. ADD THE LEMON JUICE AND WHITE WINE CONSTANTLY STIRRING. LOWER THE HEAT TO LOW MAKE SURE LIQUID IS NOT BOILING, NOW SLOWLY ADD THE 4 TABLESPOONS OF BUTTER A LITTLE AT A TIME CONSTANTLY STIRRING UNTIL ALL THE BUTTER IS MIXED IN THE SAUCE. REMOVE FROM HEAT AND SET ASIDE IF YOU ARE NOT USING IT RIGHT NOW. CAN BE REHEATED ON LOW HEAT AND CONSTANTLY STIRRING.

TRUFFLE CRÈME VINAGARETTE

½ CUP GOLDEN OR CLEAR BALSAMIC VINAGER

1 CUP OLIVE OIL

2 TABLESPOONS TRUFFLE OIL

½ CUP CRÈME FRAICHE

COMBINE ALL INGREDIENTS IN A SAUCE PAN AND **(HEAT ONLY)** OVER LOW HEAT

DEEP FRIED LEEK STRINGS

2 LEEKS

1 TABLESPOON KOSHER OR SEA SALT

3 CUPS VEGATABLE OR CANOLA OIL

CUT THE GREEN PORTION AND THE ROOT END OFF THE LEEKS. CUT THE LEEKS IN VERY THIN SLINCE LENTHWAYS AND PUT THEM IN COLD WATER TO CLEAN ANY SAND THAT MAYBE ON THEM. REMOVE THE LEEKS AND DRY ON PAPER TOWELS OR DISH RAGS. **MAKE SURE THEY ARE TOTALLY DRY BEFORE PUTTING THEM INTO THE OIL.**

FILL A LARGE POT LESS THAN HALF WITH THE OIL AND HEAT TO 350 DEGREES. ADD THE DRY LEEKS A LITTLE AT A TIME UNTIL THEY ARE GOLDEN BROWN. REMOVE THE LEEKS, PUT ON PAPER TOWELS AND SPRINKLE EACH BATCH WITH THE SALT.

AGAIN BE CAREFUL IF THE OIL LOOKS LIKE IT IS FOAMING UP WITH THE LEEKS IN THE POT REMOVE THE POT FROM THE HEAT UNTIL THE FOAM STOPS.

MAIN COURSES

LAMB MEATBALL DINNER

1 LB GROUND LAMB

1 LB GROUND VEAL

1 LB GROUND PORK

1 TEASPOON MINCED GARLIC

½ CUP MINCED ONION

1 CUP BREADCRUMBS

¾ CUP MILK

2 EGGS

½ CUP PARM CHEESE

2 TABLESPOONS PARSLEY

1 ½ TEASPOONS SALT

½ TEASPOON PEPPER

MIX ALL INGREDIENTS AND FORM INTO GOLF BALL SIZE BALLS. COOK ON COOKIE SHEET WITH PARCHMENT PAPER AT 400 DEGRESS FOR ABOUT 12 TO 15 MINUTES SERVE WITH MARINARA SAUCE AND TOP WITH PARMISAN CHEESE.

ALSO CAN BE SERVED WITH ANY PASTA OR RICE.

RAGU AND PASTA

1/2 LB GROUND VEAL

1/2 LB GROUND PORK

1/2 LB GROUND BEEF

1 TABLESPOON MINCED GARLIC

1 TABLESPOON MINCED ONION

3 TABLESPOONS PARSLEY **(LEAVES ONLY)** CHOPPED FINELY

1 TEASPOON KOSHER OR SEA SALT

1 TEASPOON BLACK PEPPER

3 CUPS MARINARA SAUCE **(RECEIPE IN COOK BOOK)**

1CUP PARMISAN CHEESE

2 TABLESPOONS OLIVE OIL

HEAT OLIVE OIL IN SKILLET ON MEDIUM HEAT. WHEN HOT, ADD THE THREE MEATS, SALT AND PEPPER AND STIR UNTIL THE MEAT IS ALL BROKEN UP. ADD THE GARLIC AND THE ONIONS AND COOK UNTIL THE MEAT IS NICE AND BROWN BUT NOT BURNT. ADD THE MARINARA SAUCE AND COOK FOR ANOTHER 20 – 25 MINUTES ON MEDIUMN HEAT. REMOVE FROM HEAT AND ADD HALF THE PARSLEY AND THE CHEESE AND STIR.

WHILE THE MEAT IS COOKING COOK YOUR FAVORITE PASTA A LITTLE, AS WE SAY "TO THE BITE", NOT SOFT. DRAIN THE PASTA AND PUT THE PASTA IN THE SKILLET WITH THE MEAT BACK ON MEDIMUN HEAT. STIR THE PASTA. SERVE AND ADD THE REST OF THE CHEESE AND PARSLEY TO INDIVIDUAL DISHES.

YOU CAN USE ANY PASTA THAT YOU LIKE

ROASTED DUCK BREAST WITH BERNAISE SAUCE

2 DUCK BREASTS DEFROSTED

1 LARGE LEEK

1 HEAD BOK CHOY

¼ TEASPOON KOSHER OR SEA SALT

¼ TEASPOON WHITE PEPPER

½ POUND RED SKIN POTATOES

BERNAISE SAUCE **(RECIPE IN COOKBOOK ON PAGE 61)**

PREPARATION OF ITEMS

LEEK- CUT ALL THE GREEN STEM OFF AND DISCARD. CUT THE END OF THE ROOT OFF. SLICE THE LEEK LENGTH WAYS VERY THIN DOWN THE MIDDLE INTO STRINGS. PUT THE LEEKS IN COLD WATER TO REMOVE ANY SAND THAT MIGHT BE INSIDE EACH STRING. LET SOAK FOR ABOUT 20 MINUTES, DRAIN AND WRAP THE LEEK STRINGS IN PAPER TOWELS TO REMOVE ALL THE WATER THEN SET ASIDE.

BOK CHOY-REMOVE ROOT END AND SOAK THE BOK CHOY ON COLD WATER TO REMOVE ANY DIRT. CUT OFF ABOUT 2 INCHES OF THE TOP GREEN LEAFS. SLICE DOWN THE MIDDLE OF EACH LEAF AND THEN CUT SMALL PIECES LENGTH WAYS AND SET ASIDE.

RED SKIN POTATOES-WASH OUTSIDE SKIN AND CUT INTO QUARTERS.

DUCK-MAKE SURE DUCK IS FULLY DEFROSTED, TAKE A SHARP KNIFE AND CUT LENGTH WAYS THROUGH THE FAT, **DO NOT CUT THROUGH THE MEAT**. NOW CUT AGAIN BUT ACROSS THE BREAST. **AGAIN DO NOT CUT INTO THE MEAT.**

COOKING OF ABOVE ITEMS

POTATOES- WRAP POTATOES IN ALUMIUM FOIL WITH OLIVE OIL SALT AND PEPPER TO TASTE. PUT FOIL ON COOKIE SHEET AND ROAST IN OVEN AT 350 DEGRESS FOR ABOUT 25 MINUTES OR UNTIL TENDER.

BOK CHOY-COOK BOK CHOY IN A SKILLET WITH TABLESPOON UNSALTED BUTTER AND 2 TABLESPOONS OLIVE OIL ON MEDIUM HEAT UNTIL TENDER.

LEEKS- IN A DEEP POT FILL POT HALF WAY WITH VEGATABLE OIL OR CANOLLIA OIL.**(DO NOT USE OLIVE OIL.)** BRING OIL TO 350 DEGRESS AND SLOWLY ADD THE STRINGS OF LEEKS A LITTLE AT A TIME. YOU MIGHT SEE THE OIL START TO FOAM UP JUST TAKE IT OFF THE HEAT UNTIL THE FOAM STOPS THEN CONTINUE COOKING AT 350. WHEN CRISPY REMOVE FROM OIL PUT ON PAPER TOWELS AND SPRINKLY WITH SALT. CONTINUE UNTIL ALL THE LEEKS ARE COOKED.

IN A VERY HOT SKILLER PUT THE DUCK FAT SIDE DOWN AND DONOT TOUCH OR MOVE THE BREAST. THE SKIN SHOULD BE DARK. WHEN DARK FLIP THE BREAST OVER ON THE MEAT SIDE AND PUT IN A 350 DEGREE OVEN FOR ABOUT 15 MINUTES FOR MEDIMUM RARE. LONGER IF YOU WANT IT COOKED FURTHER.

REMOVE THE DUCK AND PUT ON A SCREEN AND LET STAND FOR ABOUT 5-10 MINUTES FOR THE JUICES TO RETURN TO THE MEAT. NOW CUT ON AN ANGLE ¼ INCH PIECES ARRANGE ON THE PLATE WITH THE POTATOES, BOK CHOY, PUT THE LEEK STRINGS ON TOP OF THE DUCK AND THEN THE BERNAISE SAUCE.

NOTE: YOU CAN USE ANY ONE OF THE SAUCES LISTED IN THIS COOKBOOK, IT ALL DEPENDS ON YOUR TASTE

SHRIMP WITH CHERRY TOMATO SAUCE

4 LARGE SHRIMP **(PER PERSON) DESHELLED AND DEVAINED**

2 EGGS SCRAMBLED

2 TEASPOONS KOSHER OR SEA SALT

2TEASPOONS WHITE PEPPER

2 CUPS ALL PURPOSE FLOUR

2 CUPS VEGATABLE OR CANOLA OIL

FOLLOW RECEIPE FOR THE SAUCE ON PAGE 19.

PUT THE FLOUR IN A BOWL WITH HALF THE SALT AND HALF THE PEPPER. PUT THE SCRAMBLED EGGS IN ANOTHER DISH ALONG WITH THE REST OF THE SALT AND PEPPER.

HEAT OIL IN SKILLET OVER MEDIUM-HIGH HEAT.

DIP THE SHRIMP IN FLOUR, THEN EGG, THEN FLOUR AGAIN AND ADD TO THE HOT OIL. COOK THE SHRIMP FOR 3 MINUTES ON EACH SIDE THEN REMOVE FROM THE PAN AND SPRINKLE WITH A LITTLE BIT OF SALT.

ARRANGE SHRIMP ON EACH PLATE AND TOP WITH THE CHERRY SAUCE.

NOTE: YOU CAN SERVE WITH PASTA OR RICE ALSO IF YOU DESIRE.

SHRIMP WITH APRICOT SAUCE

4 LARGE SHRIMP **(4 PER PERSON)** DESHELLED AND DEVAINED

1 SMALL JAR APRICOT PRESERVE

4 TABLESPOONS APRICOT BRANDY

4 SLICES BACON **(COOK UNTIL CRISPY)** CUT IN SMALL PIECES AND SET ASIDE

1/2 TEASPOON KOSHER OR SEA SALT

1/2 TEASPOON WHITE PEPPER

2 CUPS ALL PURPOSE FLOUR

2 EGGS SCRAMBLED

4 TABLESPOONS UNSALTED BUTTER

2 TABLESPOONS OLIVE OIL

JUICE AND ZEST OF 1 LEMON

MIX FLOUR WITH HALF THE SALT AND PEPPER. MIX THE EGGS WITH THE REST OF THE SALT AND PEPPER. NOW DIP EACH SHRIMP IN THE FLOUR AND THEN THE EGG, THEN THE FLOUR AGAIN AND SET ASIDE ON A RACK. HEAT THE OIL AND BUTTER IN A LARGE SKILLET. WHEN HOT ADD THE SHRIMP GENTLY TO AVOID SPLATTERING. COOK THE SHRIMP FOR 3 MINUTES ON BOTH SIDES. ADD THE LEMON JUICE, BACON, THE JAR OF APRICOT PRESERVE AND THE BRANDY. BRING TO A LOW BOIL STIRRING CONSTANTLY UNTIL THICKENED. SPRINKLE WITH THE ZEST WHEN SERVING.

SERVE 4 PER PLATE WITH ANY SIDES YOU WANT, THAT IS YOUR CHOICE.

CLAMS IN ORANGE AND BEER SAUCE

1 DOZ CLAMS **(CHERRY STONE OR MAHOGANY CLAMS)**

1 BOTTLE BEER **(YOUR CHOSE)**

1 LARGE SHALLOT **-(FINELY DICED)**

2 CLOVES OF GARLIC **– (FINELY CHOPPED)**

JUICE AND ZEST OF 2 ORANGES

2 TABLESPOONS PARSLEY **(NO STEMS)**

2 TABLESPOONS CRÈME FRAICHE

4 TABLESPOONS GARLIC AIOLI **(RECEIPE ON PAGE 26)**

4 TABLESPOONS OLIVE OIL

IN A SAUCE PAN ADD THE OLIVE OIL ON MEDIUM HIGH HEAT. ADD GARLIC AND SHALLOTS, WAIT A FEW MINUTES THEN ADD THE CLAMS. COVER THE PAN COOK FOR A FEW MINUTES. UNCOVER AND ADD THE BEER, NOW ON MEDIUM HEAT COVER UNTIL THE CLAMS ARE ALL OPEN. NOW ADD THE ORANGE JUICE AND THE ZEST, THE CRÈME FRAICHE AND PARSLEY.

MAKE TOAST AND SPREAD THE TOAST WITH THE GARLIC AIOLI. USE THE BREAD AS DIPPING BREAD IN THE SAUCE.

YOU CAN SUBSTITUTE MUSSELS, SHRIMP, SCALLOPS OR ANY TYPE OF FISH.

DIVER SCALLOPS, WILD RICE, BOK CHOY, TOPPED WITH RASBERRY/MUSTARD SAUCE

4 LARGE SCALLOPS **(MUSSEL REMOVED)**

3 STALKS BOK CHOY CUT THINLY

1 SHALLOT CUT FINELY

1 CUP COOKED WILD RICE

2 TABLESPOONS RASBERRY/MUSTARD SAUCE

2 TABLESPOONS OLIVE OIL

¼ TEASPOON KOSHER OR SEA SALT

¼ TEASPOON WHITE PEPPER

BEFORE COOKING SCALLOPS CHECK EACH SCALLOP ON THE SIDE THERE MAY BE A THICK HARD PIECE, JUST REMOVE IT. SOME MIGHT NOT HAVE ANY ON THEM. PAT THE SCALLOPS DRY AND SET ASIDE.

IN A FRYING PAN ADD THE OLIVE OIL ON MEDIUM HEAT AND ADD THE BOK CHOY, SALT AND PEPPER AND COOK FOR ABOUT 2-3 MINUTES LEAVING THE BOK CHOY CRUNCKY. LEAVE ON VERY LOW HEAT JUST TO KEEP IT WARM. WARM UP THE COOKED WILD RICE AND SET ASIDE.

IN A DRY TEFLON FRYING PAN, HEAT ON HIGH HEAT. SALT AND PEPPER THE SCALLOPS ON BOTH SIDES. WHEN THE PAN IS VERY HOT, PUT THE SCALLOPS IN THE PAN AND DO NOT MOVE UNTIL YOU ARE READY TO FLIP THEM, ABOUT 3 MINUTES EACH SIDE.

REMOVE FROM HEAT PLACE ON A DISH WITH THE RICE AND BOK CHOY AND DRESS WITH THE RASBERRY MUSTARD SAUCE

THE RASBERRY/MUSTARD SAUCE RECEIPE IS ON PAGE 32 IN THE BOOK

DUCK LEG CONFIT WITH PASTA IN A MARINARA SAUCE

4 DUCK LEGS

1 PINT DUCK FAT OR 1 PINT VEGATABLE OIL

¼ TEASPOON KOSHER OR SEA SALT

¼ TEASPOON BLACK PEPPER

MARINARA SAUCE **(RECEIPE IN THIS BOOK ON PAGE 33)**

1 LB OF PASTA **(YOUR CHOICE)**

IN A LARGE POT ADD THE OIL. SALT AND PEPPER THE DUCK LEGS. PUT THE LEGS IN THE OIL AND HEAT THE OIL ON MEDIUM LOW HEAT. (DO NOT BRING THE OIL TO A BOIL) IF STARTING TO BOIL REDUCE HEAT, COVER AND LET SIMMER FOR 4-5 HOURS. REMEMBER LOW HEAT.

AFTER 4-5 HOURS REMOVE THE POT FROM THE STOVE AND LET COOL. IN A PLASTIC CONTAINER WITH A LID PUT THE LEGS IN THE CONTAINER AND COVER THE LEGS WITH THE COOKING OIL, MAKING SURE THE LEGS ARE FULLY COVERED.**(MAKE SURE THE OIL IS COOL TO THE TOUCH.) LET SIT IN REFRIGERATOR OVERNIGHT.**

NEXT DAY REMOVE THE DUCK FROM THE OIL; WIPE THE OIL OFF THE LEGS, **DO NOT RINSE.** STRIP THE MEAT FROM THE BONES AND HEAT THE MEAT IN THE MARINARA SAUCE.

COOK YOUR FAVORITE PASTA AND POUR SAUCE AND MEAT OVER THE PASTA.

CHICKEN BREAST WITH WHITE WINE SAUCE

2 BONELESS/SKINLESS CHICKEN BREAST

4 TABLESPOONS OLIVE OIL

2 TABLESPOONS FLOUR

2 EGGS WISKED

1 TEASPOON KOSHER OR SEA SALT

1 TEASPOON WHITE PEPPER

1 CUP BREAD CRUMBS **(ANY WILL DO)**

WRAP EACH BREAST IN SARAN AND POUND EACH ONE UNTIL EVENLY FLAT. WISK THE EGGS IN A BOWL ADD HALF THE SALT AND PEPPER. PUT THE BREAD CRUMBS IN A SEPARATE BOWL. TAKE THE CHICKEN BREASTS AND ADD THE REMAINING SALT AND PEPPER TO EACH SIDE OF THE BREAST. NOW FLOUR EACH BREAST AND DIP IN THE EGGS COVERING BOTH SIDES AND THEN PUT IN THE BREAD CRUMBS AGAIN.

IN A FRYING PAN ADD OLIVE OIL ON MEDIUM HEAT. WHEN OIL IS HOT, ADD THE BREAST TO THE PAN. LEAVE IT ALONE UNTIL THE BREAD CRUMBS LOOK BROWN **(NOT BURNT)**, ABOUT 3-5 MINUTES. NOW FLIP THE BREAST ON THE OTHER SIDE AND COOK FOR ANOTHER 5 MINUTES OR UNTIL THE TEMPERATURE OF THE INSIDE OF THE BREAST REACHES 160 DEGREES.

FOR THE WHITE WINE SAUCE FOLLOW THE RECEIPE ON PAGE 44

CHICKEN BREAST WITH TRUFFLE CRÈME VINAGARETTE

2 BONELESS/SKINLESS CHICKEN BREAST

4 TABLESPOONS OLIVE OIL

2 TABLESPOONS FLOUR

2 EGGS WISKED

1 TEASPOON KOSHER OR SEA SALT

1 TEASPOON WHITE PEPPER

1 CUP BREAD CRUMBS **(ANY WILL DO)**

WRAP EACH BREAST IN SARAN AND POUND EACH ONE UNTIL EVENLY FLAT. WISK THE EGGS IN A BOWL ADD HALF THE SALT AND PEPPER. PUT THE BREAD CRUMBS IN A SEPARATE BOWL. TAKE THE CHICKEN BREASTS AND SPRINKLE THE REMAINING SALT AND PEPPER TO EACH SIDE OF THE BREAST. NOW FLOUR EACH BREAST AND DIP IN THE EGGS COVERING BOTH SIDES AND THEN PUT IN THE BREAD CRUMBS.

IN A FRYING PAN ADD THE OLIVE OIL ON MEDIUM HEAT. WHEN OIL IS HOT, ADD THE BREAST TO THE PAN. LEAVE IT ALONE UNTIL THE BREAD CRUMBS LOOK BROWN **(NOT BURNT).** ABOUT 3-5 MINUTES. NOW FLIP THE BREAST ON THE OTHER SIDE AND COOK FOR ANOTHER 5 MINUTES OR UNTIL THE TEMPERATURE OF THE INSIDE OF THE BREASTS REACHES 160 DEGREES.

FOR THE TRUFFLE SAUCE SEE PAGE 62 IN THE COOK BOOK

PORK TENDERLOIN WITH PORT WINE SAUCE

1 SMALL PORT TENDERLOIN

½ TEASPOON KOSHER OR SEA SALT

½ TEASPOON BLACK PEPPER

½ TEASPOON GRANULATED GARLIC POWDER

½ TEASPOON POWDERED ONION

4 TABLESPOONS OLIVE OIL

1 TABLESPOON UNSALTED BUTTER

PORT WINE SAUCE **(RECEIPE ON PAGE 38 IN THE BOOK)**

UNWRAP THE TENDERLOIN AND REMOVE ALL THE SILVER SKIN FROM THE PORK TENDERLOIN. LEAVE THE REGULAR FAT ON THE MEAT. COMBINE THE SALT, PEPPER GARLIC AND ONION POWDER IN A BOWL. RUB THE TENDERLOIN WITH THE SALT MIXTURE ALL OVER THE MEAT AND LET REST AT ROOM TEMPERATURE FOR ABOUT 10-20 MINUTES.

TURN OVEN ON TO 350 DEGREES. IN A FRYING PAN HEAT OLIVE OIL AND BUTTER ON MEDIUM HIGH HEAT. WHEN THE PAN IS HOT PUT THE MEAT IN THE PAN IT SHOULD BE SIZZLING, DO NOT TOUCH THE MEAT LEAVE IT ALONE. IN ABOUT 5 MINUTES TURN THE MEAT OVER, **BUT DO NOT USE A FORK**, USE A PAIR OF TONGS. AFTER 5 MINUTES, TURN THE MEAT OVER ON BOTH SIDES TO SEAL THE ENDS. PUT THE PAN WITH THE MEAT IN THE OVEN ON MIDLE RACK AND COOK UNTIL THE INTERNAL TEMPERATURE READS 160 DEGREES, LESS IF YOU WANT IT PINK INSIDE THEN 150 DEGREES.

REMOVE THE MEAT FROM THE OVEN AND PLACE ON A DISH AND LET IT COOL FOR ABOUT 10 MINUTES TO DRAW THE JUICES BACK INTO THE MEAT.

CUT THE MEAT ANYWAY YOU LIKE AND SERVE WITH AND VEGATABLE AND POTATO OF YOUR CHOICE. TOP THE MEAT WITH THE PORT WINE SAUCE.

SEA BASS WITH SMOKED SALMON SAUCE

(1) 6 OZ PORTION SEA BASS **(REMOVE ANY BONES)**

4 TABLESPOONS OLIVE OIL

2 TABLESPOONS UNSALTED BUTTER

½ TEASPOON KOSHER OR SEA SALT

½ TEASPOON WHITE PEPPER

SMOKED SALMON SAUCE **(RECIPE ON PAGE 59 IN THE BOOK)**

PREHEAT YOUR OVEN TO 400 DEGREES. IN A FRYING PAN, ADD THE OIL AND BUTTER AND MELT OVER MEDIMUN HIGH HEAT. PUT THE BASS IN THE PAN AND COOK FOR ABOUT 4 MINUTES. TURN BASS OVER ON THE OTHER SIDE AND PUT INTO THE OVEN AND COOK FOR ANOTHER 4 MINUTES. REMOVE FROM OVEN, ADD POTATOES, RICE, VEGATABLES OR ANYTHING YOU DESIRE AND THEN TOP WITH THE SAUCE.

YOU CAN SUBSTITUTE ANY TYPE OF FISH THAT YOU DESIRE

SEA BASS WITH WASABI CRÈME FRAICHE

(1) 6 OZ PORTION SEA BASS **(MAKE SURE THERE ARE NO BONES REMOVE IF ANY)**

4 TABLESPOONS OLIVE OIL

2 TABLESPOONS UNSALTED BUTTER

½ TEASPOON KOSHER OR SEA SALT

½ TEASPOON WHITE PEPPER

WASABI CRÈME FRAICHE SAUCE **(RECEIPE ON PAGE 58 IN THE BOOK)**

PREHEAT YOUR OVEN AT 400 DEGREES. IN A FRYING PAN ADD THE OIL AND BUTTER AND MELT OVER MEDIMUN HIGH HEAT. PUT THE BASS IN THE PAN AND COOK FOR ABOUT 4 MINUTES. AFTER THAT TURN BASS OVER ON THE OTHER SIDE AND PUT INTO THE OVEN AND COOK FOR ANOTHER 4 MINUTES. REMOVE FROM OVEN ADD POTATOES, RICE, VEGATABLES OR ANYTHING YOU DESIRE AND THEN TOP WITH THE SAUCE.

YOU CAN SUBSTITUTE ANY TYPE OF FISH THAT YOU DESIRE

RACK OF LAMB WITH PORT WINE SAUCE

1 RACK OF LAMB

1 CARROT – PEELED AND CUT IN QUARTERS

1 RED ONION-PEELED AND CUT IN QUARTERS

1 CELERY STALK- CUT IN HALF

½ CUP DIJON MUSTARD

½ CUP PURE HONEY

¼ TEASPOON KOSHER OR SEA SALT

¼ TEASPOON WHITE PEPPER

1 TABLESPOON OLIVE OIL

1 TABLESPOON UNSALTED BUTTER

PREPARING THE LAMB: REMOVE THE LAMB FROM THE PLASTIC WRAPPER, WITH A SHARP KNIFE REMOVE THE SILVER SKIN IS VERY CAREFULLY NOT TO CUT INTO THE FLESH. THE MAIN FAT TOWARDS THE BONES LEAVE ATTACHED.

MIX THE MUSTARD AND THE HONEY IN A BOWL AND SET ASIDE. HAVE THE CARROTS, ONION AND CELERY READY TO GO.

PREPARE THE SAUCE: I WOULD USE EITHER THE PORT WINE SAUCE ON PAGE 51 OR THE BERNAISE ON PAGE 56. KEEP THE SAUCE WARM BUT DO NOT BOIL.

PREHEAT OVEN TO 400 DEGREES. IN A LARGE FRYING PAN HEAT THE OIL AND BUTTER UNTIL MELTED AND HOT. SPRINKLE THE LAMB WITH THE SALT AND PEPPER AND PLACE IN THE PAN, MEAT SIDE DOWN AND LEAVE IT ALONE AFTER 3 MINUTES TURN THE RACK BONE SIDE DOWN IN THE PAN AND REMOVE AFTER 2 MINUTES AND NOW RUB THE ENTIRE LAMB EXCEPT THE BONES WITH THE HONEY AND MUSTARD MIXTURE. NOW ADD THE ONION, CELERY AND CARROT TO THE PAN AND PUT THE LAMB BACK IN THE PAN AND PUT IN THE OVEN. WITH

ANY THERMOMETER COOK THE LAMB TO 155 DEGREES FOR RAW, 160 DEGREES FOR MEDIMUN RAW. **ANYTHING AFTER THAT TEMPERATURE FORGET IT.**

DISCARD THE ONION AND CARROT AND CELERY.

REMOVE AND LET COOL FOR 5 MINUTES. THEN CUT IN SINGLE PORTIONS. JUST FOLLOW THE BONE DOWN TO THE END.

SERVE WITH ANY VEGATABLE AND POTATO, RICE OR ANYTHING ELSE YOU DESIRE.

BEEF SKEWERS WITH ORANGE LEMON GARLIC AND GINGER

4 TABLESPOONS WHITE WINE

3 TABLESPOONS OLIVE OIL

4 GARLIC CLOVES FINELY CHOPPED

ZEST AND JUICE OF 1 ORANGE

ZEST AND JUICE OF 1 LEMON

3 TABLESPOONS GINGER CHOPPED FINELY

1 LB OF BEEF (RUMP STEAK) CUBED

1 LB BABY ONIONS PEELED AND HALVED

2 BELL PEPPERS SEEDED AND CUT IN CUBES **(RED, YELLOW OR ORANGE PEPPERS)**

1 PACKAGE OF CHERRY TOMATOES

½ TABLESPOON KOSHER OR SEA SALT

½ TABLESPOON BLACK PEPPER

MIX THE WINE, OLIVE OIL, ORANGE ZEST AND JUICE, THE LEMON ZEST AND JUICE AND GARLIC. IN A PLASTIC CONTAINER PUT THE MEAT AND THE ABOVE ITEMS IN AND MARINATE IN THE REFRIGERATOR FOR 6-8 HOURS.

REMOVE THE MEAT FROM THE MARINADE. PUT THE MEAT, TOMATOES, ONIONS AND PEPPERS ON THE SKEWERS.

EITHER IN THE OVEN BROILER OR ON THE OUTSIDE BARBARQUE COOK THE SKEWERS FOR ABOUT 5 MINUTES, TURNING EVERY FEW MINUTES.

SERVE WITH WILD RICE.

YOU CAN SUBSTITUTE LAMB, SHRIMP, SCALLOPS OR KEEP IT TOTALLY VEGATARIAN

CHICKEN ROLLATINI WITH MARINARA SAUCE

4 SKINLESS, BONELESS CHICKEN BREAST

4 TABLESPOONS GARLIC CHOPPED VERY FINE

2 TABLESPOONS KOSHER OR SEA SALT

2 TABLESPOONS WHITE PEPPER

4 SLICES COLD CUT HAM SLICED THIN

4 SLICES OF PROVOLONE CHEESE SLICED THIN

MARINARA SAUCE **(RECEIPE ON PAGE 46 IN THE BOOK)**

½ CUP OLIVE OIL

2 EGGS WISKED

1 CUP FLOUR

TOOTHPICKS

FIRST PREPARE THE MARINARA SAUCE AND SET ASIDE.

PREPPING THE CHICKEN: REMOVE ALL FAT FROM CHICKEN, PUT EACH PIECE IN PLASTIC WRAP BOTH UNDER AND OVER THE BREAST, NOW POUND THE BREAST UNTIL IT IS FLAT EVENLY, AND SET ASIDE. WISK THE EGGS IN BOWL WITH ½ TEASPOONS OF BOTH SALT AND PEPPER. IN A SEPARATE BOWL, MIX FLOUR, ½ TEASPOON OF SALT AND PEPPER AND MIX.

LAY THE CHICKEN BREAST ON A COOKIE SHEET AND SPRINKLE EACH ONE WITH SALT AND PEPPER, PUT A PIECE OF HAM AND CHEESE ON EACH ONE ALONG WITH THE GARLIC. NOW ROLL EACH BREAST AND SKEWER WITH TOOTHPICKS. ROLL EACH BREAST IN FLOUR THEN EGG THEN FLOUR AGAIN AND SET ASIDE ON A RACK.

IN A DEEP FRYING PAN OR SKILLET ADD THE OLIVE OIL AND PLACE ON MEDIUM HIGH HEAT. WHEN HOT ADD THE BREAST AND COOK UNTIL GOLDEN BROWN. REMOVE FROM PAN, ADD THE MARINARA

SAUCE AND HEAT UNTIL IT COMES TO A ROLLING BOIL. ADD THE BREASTS AND FINISH IN THE OVEN FOR ABOUT 20 -25 MINUTES AT 400 DEGREES.

CAN BE SERVED WITH ANY PASTA, POTATOES AND/OR VEGATABLES.

YOU CAN SUBSTITUTE VEAL OR STEAK, JUST FOLLOW THE DIRECTIONS FOR POUNDING THEM THIN.

STUFFED CHICKEN BREAST WITH SAGE/ HAM WITH A MUSHROOM SAUCE

4 BONELESS CHICKEN BREAST

8 SAGE LEAVES

4 SLICES OF DELI HAM SLICED THIN

1 CUP OLIVE OIL

½ TABLESPOON KOSHER OR SEA SALT

½ TABLESPOON BLACK PEPPER

1 POUND MUSHROOMS **(ANY TYPE YOU LIKE - A MIXTURE IS GOOD)** CUT IN QUARTERS

1 QUART CHICKEN STOCK **(AVAILABLE AT ANY GROCERY STORE)**

1 CUP RED DRINKING WINE

2 TABLESPOONS CHOPPED GARLIC

2 TABLESPOON CHOPPED TYME

1 TABLESPOON CHOPPED FLAT LEAF PARSLEY

1 CUP FLOUR

2 WISKED EGGS

PREPING THE CHICKEN BREAST: CUT A POCKET ON THE SIDE OF THE BREAST AND STUFF EACH ONE WITH 2 SAGE LEAVES AND A PIECE OF THE HAM AND SET ASIDE.

IN A SKILLET AND ½ THE OLIVE OIL AND HEAT ON MEDIUM HIGH HEAT. ADD THE MUSHROOMS, SALT, PEPPER AND GARLIC AND THE TYME. WHEN THE MUSHROOMS ARE GOLDEN BROWN AND THE WINE AND THE CHICKEN STOCK AND SET THE PAN ASIDE.

PUT CHICKEN IN THE FLOUR, THEN THE EGG AND THEN THE FLOUR AGAIN. IN A SKILLET ADD THE REMAINING OIL AND HEAT ON MEDIUM HEAT.

PLACE THE CHICKEN BREAST IN THE PAN AND COOK BOTH SIDES UNTIL GOLDEN BROWN AND SET ASIDE.

PUT BREASTS INTO THE PAN WITH THE MUSHROOMS AND THE STOCK AND WINE. TOP WITH THE PARSLEY

COOK IN THE OVEN AT 400 DEGREES FOR 15-20 MINUTES.

SERVE WITH PASTA OR ANY VEGATABLES YOU CHOOSE

PRESERVED LEMONS OR LIMES

6 SMALL MASON JARS

18 LEMONS OR LIMES

3 CUPS KOSHER OR SEA SALT

IN HOT BOILING WATER PUT THE JARS, LIDS AND SEALS IN THE WATER AND BOIL FOR ABOUT 10 MINUTES. REMOVE THE JARS, TOPS AND SEALS AND PLACE THE JARS TOP DOWN ON PAPER TOWELS TO DRAIN ALONG WITH THE LIDS AND SEALS. AFTER COOLING, PLACE HALF THE AMOUNT OF SALT IN THE BOTTON OF EACH JAR. CUT THE LEMONS OR LIMES IN QUARTERS AND STUF THEM IN THE JAR. CONTINUE STUFFING THEM IN THE JAR UNTIL NO MORE CAN FIT. NOW ADD THE REMAINING SALT TO THE TOP OF EACH JAR.

SQUEEZE THE REMAINING LEMONS OR LIMES UNTIL THE JUICE FILLS TO THE TOP OF THE JAR. PUT THE SEAL ON AND THE LID AND SCREW THE LID ON TIGHT.

STORE IN THE REFRIGERATOR TURNING THE JARS OVER ABOUT ONCE A WEEK FOR ABOUT 2 MONTHS. **DATE THE TOP OF THE JARS**

NOTE: WHEN YOU ARE READY TO USE ANY AMOUNT OF THE LEMONS OR LIMES, RINSE THEM BEFORE USING. CUT IN SMALL PIECES, CAN BE USED IN SALADS, COOKED WITH MUSHROOMS OR ONIONS. LET YOUR MIND RUN WILD WITH THESE. THEY BECOME VERY SWEET. LEFT IN THE REFRIGERATOR THEY WILL LASTS FOR SEVERAL MONTHS; I HAVE MINE FOR 2 YEARS AND ARE STILL GREAT.

SCALLOPS WITH LIMES AND RED PEPPER FLAKES

4 DIVER SCALLOPS

2 LIMES **(ZESTED AND JUICED)**

½ TEASPOON RED PEPPER FLAKES (**ADD MORE IF DESIRED)**

½ TEASPOON KOSHER OR SEA SALT

½ TEASPOON WHITE PEPPER

¼ CUP HEAVY CREAM

¼ CUP DRY WHITE WINE **(DRINKING WINE)**

PREPING THE SCALLOPS: ON THE SIDE OF THE SCALLOPS THERE CAN BE A HARD MEMBRAIN REMOVE IF THERE IS ONE.

ZEST AND JUICE THE LIMES AND SET ASIDE ALONG WITH THE RED PEPPER FLAKES AND HEAVY CREAM.

SALT AND PEPPER THE SCALLOPS. THEN IN A VERY HOT TEFLON SKILLET ADD THE SCALLOPS AND LEAVE THEM ALONE. DO NOT MOVE THEM. AFTER ABOUT THREE MINUTES TURN THE SCALLOPS OVER AND AFTER 2 MINUTES REDUCE THE HIGH TO MEDIUM AND ADD THE JUICE AND ZEST OF THE LIMES AND THE RED PEPPER FLAKES. AFTER ONE MINUTE MORE, ADD THE WHITE WINE AND THE HEAVY CREAM. REDUCE BY HALF.

SERVE OVER RICE, PASTA OR SERVE WITH ANY POTATOES AND VEGETABLES.

ROAST LEG OF LAMB

1 SEMI BONELESS LEG OF LAMB

3 LARGE CARROTS

3 STALKS CELERY

1 SPANISH OR YELLOW ONION

10 CLOVES PEELED GARLIC **(LEAVE HOLE)**

4 TABLESPOONS EXTRA VIRGIN OLIVE OIL

2 TABLESPOONS KOSHER OR SEA SALT

2 TABLESPOONS BLACK PEPPER

1 CUP DRINKING WHITE

PREPPING THE LAMB: TAKE A SHARP KNIFE AND CUT SLITS IN THE MEAT AND PRESS EACH GARLIC PIECE IN THE SLIT. CONTINUE ALL AROUND THE LEG UNTIL YOU HAVE PUT ALL 10 PIECES IN THE LAMB. NOW RUB THE LEG ALL OVER WITH THE OLIVE OIL FIRST THEN THE SALT AND PEPPER SALT AND PEPPER.

IN AN OVEN PAN WITH A RACK CUT THE END OF THE CARROT OFF AND CUT THE CARROTS, CELERY AND ONION IN QUARTERS AND PLACE IN THE BOTTOM OF THE PAN. PLACE THE RACK BACK IN AND PUT THE LAMB ON THE RACK.

PREHEAT THE OVEN TO 350 DEGREES. PLACE THE LAG OF LAMB IN THE OVEN. AFTER ABOUT 1 HOUR POUR ABOUT 2 CUPS OF WATER IN THE BOTTOM OF THE PAN AND RETURN THE LAMB TO THE OVEN. AFTER ANOTHER HOUR ADD 1 CUP OF DRINKING WINE IN THE PAN.

COOK THE LAMB UNTIL THE INTERNAL TEMPERATURE REACHES 155 DEGREES, REMOVE FROM OVEN AND LET STAND FOR ABOUT 20

MINUTES TO FINISH COOKING. **THIS WILL BE MEDIUM RARE.** LEAVE IN OVEN UNTIL TEMPERATURE REACHES 165 FOR MEDIUM.

PUREE THE LIQUID AND THE VEGETABLES IN BLENDER THEN ADD THE STOCK TO BROWN GRAVY.

About the Author

He has included both family and his own recipes that are very easy to prepare and also suggests what sauces or dressing to use and has included the recipes in the book and showing what pages they are on. It's a very unique cook book that covers many differ recipes.

Printed in the United States
By Bookmasters